THE POWER OF CREATIVITY

A THREE-PART SERIES FOR WRITERS, ARTISTS, MUSICIANS AND ANYONE IN SEARCH OF GREAT IDEAS

BRYAN COLLINS

BECOME A *Writer* TODAY

CONTENTS

THE POWER OF CREATIVITY
(BOOK 3)

For A.

By Bryan Collins

Become a Writer Today

PREFACE

Do you want proven and free advice that will help you become more creative and find better ideas?

If you sign up at becomeawritertoday.com/pocbonus, I'll send you a free video lesson based on this book. You'll also get exclusive excerpts from my next book about creativity.

THE POWER OF CREATIVITY (BOOK 1)

LEARNING HOW TO BUILD LASTING HABITS, FACE YOUR FEARS AND CHANGE YOUR LIFE

BRYAN COLLINS

THE POWER OF
CREATIVITY

LEARNING HOW TO BUILD
LASTING HABITS, FACE YOUR FEARS,
AND **CHANGE** YOUR LIFE
(BOOK 1)

1

THE MIRROR

"We don't see things as they are, we see them as we are."
– Anais Nin

October 17th, 2009

It was the morning after my thirtieth birthday party, and I was lying on the cold tiles in the upstairs bathroom of my house. My skin felt sticky to touch, and I imagined a shard of glassware was tearing my head in two.

I got up, put my hands on the sink, looked in the mirror and into my bloodshot eyes. I didn't like what I saw.

I could (almost) forgive myself for having a crippling hangover the morning after my birthday. I knew my life had some trappings of success: a healthy son and daughter, a wife, a paying job and a modest-sized house.

But I knew I was a failure.

However, since I was a five-year-old boy reading a tattered copy of Roald Dahl's *The BFG* underneath the bedcovers with a flashlight between my teeth, I wanted to be a writer. But to want something and to be brave enough to pursue it are two different things. I'd spent 25 years being too afraid to pursue what I wanted.

For years, I read books about getting more done, coming up with ideas, unlocking fresh thinking, changing habits, writing, and managing To Do lists, calendars and even time itself, but I was the ultimate procrastinator.

I collected other people's big ideas like they were rare coins that belonged in a glass case at the back of my mind. I never put what I found into practise. I was too afraid to start, too afraid to go after what I wanted, too afraid to think big.

Sure, some of my decisions opened doors for me. I talked about Ernest Hemingway and Anaïs Nin over pints of beer with friends, and I studied journalism in college (a suitable course for any would-be writer). I even talked my way into a job as a print journalist for a Dublin newspaper.

There, I was paid to report on news stories each week. I was terrible at it. I dreaded the weekly news meetings, and I couldn't stand being in the same room as the editor of the newspaper. I was permanently devoid of ideas to write or report on, and everybody at the paper knew it.

I didn't last long at that job or the next job in the media.

I left journalism and drifted into another career that had nothing to do with writing, a career that snuffed out any sparks of creativity from its employees with mind-numbing routines, policies and procedures.

I became afraid of taking creative chances because I was worried about paying the bills and of what others would think. I became caught up in the day-to-day practicalities of life.

So the morning after my birthday, I looked in the mirror at my receding hairline and the first flecks of grey in my beard. I saw I was no closer to becoming a writer than the five-year-old boy who stayed up at night reading a frayed, yellow copy of *The BFG*.

I realised I needed to face my fears. I was a zebra who needed to change his stripes.

I needed to at least start, and I could do it with small, incremental changes. I'd work on becoming physically and mentally healthier. I'd seek out new ideas and put them into practise. I'd get over feeling afraid of rejection and failure, and I'd learn the demands of my craft.

The Road Ahead

To be creative is to embark on a long journey. I can't promise where you'll end up, but I know where we'll start. In this book, I'll explain why keeping an orderly and quiet life will help you prepare for fantastic and wild ideas.

I'll also guide you through setting up your studio or where you work for success, the difference between efficiency and effectiveness and how to feed your subconscious.

You'll discover why knowing your guiding purpose is just as important as feeling inspired about your creative projects. You'll learn how a mentor can help you face your fears and overcome everyday obstacles. And you'll find out what to do if you can't find one.

I cannot think of anything more powerful for writers, musicians or artists than a daily creative habit. So, I'll guide you through which ones to cultivate and what to ignore.

I'll explain why strengthening your mind and body and working hard is key to fresh thinking. But what if you're feeling exhausted?

Well, you can always turn to one of your side projects like television director, producer and writer Matthew Weiner, which I'll explain later.

Finally, we'll go to war. We're going to conquer any fears you have about creativity or your craft and then move boldly forward.

In each chapter, I'll draw on scientific studies (because we can all benefit from a little science), and I'll also examine the lives of contemporary and past creative masters from the arts, business, technology and more.

Each chapter concludes with applicable exercises or "Creative Takeaways" that will help you overcome common setbacks in your work.

(Because, hey, theory is nice, but practise is better.)

Who This Book is For

It's the first in a three-part series about creativity, which I wrote for new writers, musicians, filmmakers, and artists.

This book, in particular, is for anyone who has ever thought "I have a hard time being creative" or "I would like to discover my passion" or even "the prospects of my work being rejected is terrifying".

If you're an artist adrift, I wrote this book for you.

I'm not all sunshine, rainbows and lollipops, so if you're looking for a shortcut to a six-figure paycheque or a glittering review in the *New Yorker*, get out now.

I'd love a shortcut as much as the next person, you will find none here. You're still going to have to do the hard work. As I've learned firsthand, when your eyes are bloodshot, your fingers callused and your back aching, you're still on the hook for working on your ideas, for stepping forwards.

Oh, and here's the thing:

When I read books that tackle subjects like creativity, I'm

struck by how distant the writer is from his or her research, and how dry the material reads.

It's as if a SERIOUS topic like creativity warrants objective distance and emotional detachment. Yet, reader loses when an author's detachment results in dry prose devoid of storytelling and steeped in research and critical analysis.

Regardless of whether the material between the covers is worth the slog, those books are just not much fun to read.

I don't want you to lose.

So you'll find my story, my fears, my struggles, my wins and my setbacks woven through these pages. I've put as much of myself and as many illuminating stories about habit-building, conquering your fears and nurturing your creativity into this book as possible.

But, you've been waiting long enough.

So, let's begin.

2

PREPARE TO BE INSPIRED

"I think people who create and write, it actually does flow - just flows from into their head, into their hand, and they write it down. It's simple."
– Paul McCartney

I DREAM of standing on the Cliffs of Moher, edging towards the Atlantic Ocean, the wind snapping at my skin. I dream of being surrounded by friends and family and then falling until I'm overwhelmed by the raging sea.

I dream of a restaurant lit by candles, of medium-rare filet steak, dark red Bordeaux and marijuana. I dream of eating with friends from college and us realising we have nothing to share anymore.

I dream of returning to my old job as a care worker in a hospital, being pulled aside by my ageing manager – her curly brown hair now straight and grey – and being told, "You don't know how to do this anymore Bryan, you're fired."

I dream of producing a radio show for a would-be politician and then being let go. I dream about falling forwards and of reinvention.

I dream of lying in bed next to a warm body and telling her my problems. I dream of her hands moving across the dark, of being touched and being unable to touch. I dream of standing at the top of a church putting a ring on her finger. I dream of marriage and divorce, of regret and of yesterday.

I dream of a sunny October morning, the day of the Dublin City Marathon and of being unable to find the start line. I dream of putting one foot in front of the other even though my muscles are on fire; I dream of running on until I reach the finish line.

I dream of wearing a new grey suit, of tall glass buildings in the city, of shaking my new boss's hand and starting again. I dream of six-figure paydays, of sham and drudgery, and financial ruin.

I dream of melting clocks, war, fog and smoke, steel tipped helmets and marching black leather boots, my bloody face in the dirt. I dream of holding the line. I dream of a cold Christmas morning. I wake up covered in sweat.

I've got an idea.

An Artist's Slumber

In 2008, a British radio presenter asked Paul McCartney (b. 1942) to name his favourite Beatles song. McCartney answered that he loves "Yesterday", which he recorded in 1965.

 One of mine? If I had to answer one song, it would have to be 'Yesterday' because it came

to me in a dream and because 3,000 people
are supposed to have recorded it.

That was entirely magical – I have no idea
how I wrote that. I just woke up one morning
and it was in my head. I didn't believe it for
about two weeks."

Oh to sit around on the couch or lie in bed, waiting for a
divine moment of inspiration to strike. Then to rush downstairs, open a notebook and bash out 10,000 words of great
prose that sets the world on fire or, as in McCartney's case,
scratch out a hit record that becomes the most covered song
of all time.

McCartney isn't the first creative master to turn towards
dreams for inspiration.

Spanish surrealist painter Salvador Dali (1904-1989) – he
of the narrow, upright moustache – slept as deeply and as
soundly as possible before working on his big ideas.

Dali depended on "physical and psychic calm" that a
deep, restful night's sleep brought before approaching the
white, virgin canvas and beginning a new pictorial work.

He even went as far as to influence his dreams by having
a valet pour fragrances on his pillow before waking, having
melodies play quietly in the background as he slept and
applying intense light to his pupils so he could dream in
colours.

In his book, *50 Secrets of Magic Craftsmanship,* Dali wrote
to aspiring painters:

 ..in undertaking an important pictorial work
which you are anxious to bring to a successful
completion and on which your heart is
particularly set, you must before anything else

begin it by sleeping as deeply, as soundly as possible for you to do."

After a deep night's sleep, Dali worked each morning for several hours on his surrealist paintings of melting pocket watches, distorted faces, landscapes and dream sequences.

When afternoon came, Dali returned to his subconscious mind for inspiration. He sat in a bony Spanish armchair near his painting supplies, tilted his head back and draped his hands over the arms of the chair.

In his left hand, Dali held a large heavy key, which he dangled over a plate on the floor.

As soon as Dali closed his eyes and fell asleep, his grip relaxed, he dropped the key and it landed on the plate. The crashing sound woke him, and he immediately picked up his painting supplies and recommenced painting while in a dream-like state.

Dali explained,

 And the most characteristic slumber, the one most appropriate to the exercise of the art of painting . . . is the slumber which I call 'the slumber with a key,'...you must resolve the problem of 'sleeping without sleeping,' which is the essence of the dialectics of the dream, since it is a repose which walks in equilibrium on the taut and invisible wire which separates sleeping from waking."

At first glance, stories like these give the illusion of the creative process being quick and easy and altogether alien from the grind and monotony of daily hard work.

Look more closely at these moments of inspiration, and

you'll discover idling about or waiting until an idea arrives is not how masterpieces get made.

Creative masters like McCartney and Dali are able to recognise inspiration and then act on it only because they've spent hours turning up and doing the work beforehand.

They've fertilised the soil and seeded their ideas long in advance. Such masters are intimately familiar with the tools of their craft, and they've spent time shaping fragile concepts of big ideas.

In an interview with *Paste Magazine*, McCartney said,

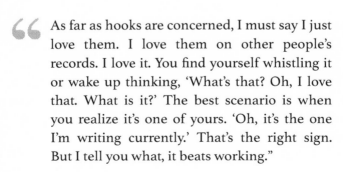 [Songs] definitely just arrive out of thin air, but I think you have to know how to spot them. I think someone building a car suddenly knows when the design is right or when the engine sounds good. After a while you get used to that, and you say, 'Yeah, this is the way you go.'"

McCartney doesn't just wait for ideas for hit songs to appear out of thin air. He also gets ideas for song hooks by constantly considering how others compose and then by developing his idea to spot those hooks in the wild.

As far as hooks are concerned, I must say I just love them. I love them on other people's records. I love it. You find yourself whistling it or wake up thinking, 'What's that? Oh, I love that. What is it?' The best scenario is when you realize it's one of yours. 'Oh, it's the one I'm writing currently.' That's the right sign. But I tell you what, it beats working."

In Dali's book referenced above, he provides new artists with a schedule they must follow.

If you're wrestling with an idea for a masterpiece, he recommends turning up before the virgin canvas each morning at eight o'clock and working for at least five and a half hours, six days a week until your masterpiece is complete.

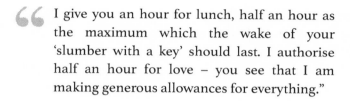

> I give you an hour for lunch, half an hour as the maximum which the wake of your 'slumber with a key' should last. I authorise half an hour for love – you see that I am making generous allowances for everything."

Dali continues:

> I guarantee you that if with the five and a half hours that I give you to fill in the landscape or sea you do not have enough...you are not the great painter of genius that you claim to be and your work will not be the masterpiece we expected from your brush."

For McCartney and Dali, the creative process is as much about preparation and good habits as it is about moments of inspiration.

Creative masters keep a schedule, they treat their work seriously, and get to it whether they're inspired or not. You too can cultivate creative habits that change your life, and here's how.

Sacrifice the Non-Essentials

So you want to build lasting habits that change your life?

Well, you might enjoy sitting down on the couch each evening to watch a comedy or a film or even play a video game, but now things are different. You will replace old habits with productive activities.

You won't have as much free time as you used too. You must commit to spending some of your free hours alone in your room or studio, even if a boss or lover wants to know what you're doing.

Are you prepared to sacrifice watching television, playing games, spending time on social media, reading trashy books, enjoying late nights out or pursuing side projects that have nothing to do with your creative passions?

Because when you sacrifice the non-essential parts of your day, you'll gain the momentum you need to progress your big ideas.

Tame Your Environment

If you're not in the habit of keeping a creative schedule, you'll encounter mental resistance when you try to do your work. Go easy on yourself by setting up an office or studio with mental triggers.

Remove anything from this environment that distracts, for example, television or a games console. You could even go as far as disconnecting Internet access in advance.

Willpower is a finite resource, and you don't want to expend it wrestling with distractions.

Remove anything from your environment that has nothing to do with your big ideas. Leave visual clues about your work and ideas. Write notes to yourself each night about what to work on the next day.

Ease Yourself into It

To cultivate lasting creative habits, prepare your work in advance. This practice ensures starting work each day takes a minimum amount of effort.

If you're writing a book chapter, for example, open the chapter in your computer, connect your headphones and queue your writing music in advance. This way, upon waking each morning, you'll know what to do immediately without thinking about it.

You can also ease yourself in by spending 10 or 15 minutes reviewing the previous day's work, reading, doodling or admiring the work of others who inspire you.

Like stretches help an athlete warm up, this will help you become more intimate with your ideas faster.

Create Space

Working on your big ideas can be messy, but you need a clear space to create this mess in the first place.

When you finish working for the day, reset your work-space and sort through what you've worked on. Just as a master craftsman puts away his tools after work, you must tidy your desk or studio, file your notes and reorganise everything.

Then, lay out the following day's work and ideas and the tools you need before you go to bed.

Become More Efficient

The creative process is sometimes sloppy and disorganised.

Both good ideas and bad ideas appear at unusual times like at 03:23. They arrive in unexpected places too, like in the shower. So, you must be efficient about your routine.

To do this, anticipate what you need and then arrange everything so it's to hand. Organise your tools and your supplies so that everything is in one place that you can easily access.

Then, check that you have everything you need such as pens, pencils, paints, paper, books, your notes, a firm resolve etc. before you start working.

You don't want to waste time looking for your notes, research or buying supplies online when you could be working on a big idea.

Become More Effective

Dali recommends artists set a goal of painting their master-piece by working six days a week, but what if this practice is too ambitious?

Open up your calendar, set a deadline for your creative project and, working backwards, block out time on your calendar each day to create. Then hold yourself accountable to this routine.

At the end of the week or month, review your routine. Ask yourself how many new ideas you came up with and whether you're hitting your target word count or putting in enough hours in front of the canvas or page.

If you find your creative project isn't on track, consider what's holding you back and how you can remove these blocks. Get outside help from somebody who will hold you accountable if you must. Only renegotiate your deadlines as a last resort.

Nudge Yourself Along

If you can't write for an hour today, sit down and write for 15 minutes. If you don't have enough energy to paint or write after work, try for just five minutes in the morning.

If you're feeling anxious about emailing interview requests for your documentary, just draft the email and gather the addresses you need.

If you're a writer, turn up in front of the blank page at the same time every day and force yourself to write even if you've got nothing to say. I like to start with a short journal entry about my intentions for the day or re-read the previous day's work.

If you're a filmmaker, go to the set or your script and figure out how you're going to approach the next scene in a fresh way.

You will make steady but determined progress towards your goal if you nudge your big ideas along in some small way each day.

Feed Your Subconscious

Before I go to bed, I read a section of what I worked on that day. I hold this thought in my mind for a few seconds before going to sleep. I do this because keeping an idea in my mind passes it over to my subconscious, which will continue to work on the idea while I sleep.

When I wake the next morning, I try to remember what I dreamt. I write this down quickly before it disappears from my mind.

Afterwards, I make a conscious effort to get to do at least an hour's work before I eat and get ready for the day, as I want to catch the ideas of my subconscious while they linger and before the demands of the day take over.

If you're going to use this approach, hold an image of what you want to accomplish firmly in your mind before you drift to sleep. It should be something specific, like a particular section of your book or a verse in a song you're writing.

Reward Yourself

The Hindu spiritual text, the Bhagavad Gita tells us, "You have the right to work, but never to the fruit of work. You should never engage in action for the sake of reward, nor should you long for inaction."

So, it's no surprise that creative masters feel motivated to continue even if they're working alone or progress is slow.

One of the best ways to foster this inner motivation is to mark small victories, like keeping a new creative routine or reaching a little milestone such as a targeted word-count or a finished painting.

You can mark these milestones by taking a trip to a museum, a walk in the park, a lie in on the weekends or by enjoying a night out with friends.

The goal here isn't to work on an idea solely for a reward; it's to build a mental link between your new creative routine and positive experiences.

Commit to Your Ideas

You can't count on creativity to appear at will; it takes months or even years to develop the mental resources you need to come up with or recognise quality ideas consistently, but here's the thing:

Turning up every day sends a signal to your subconscious that you're dedicated to the virgin canvas, the blank page or your medium of choice.

Like a long-distance runner training for the Olympics, by turning up each day, you prepare your mind and body for your creative, hard work.

Then, when an idea arrives in a dream or when inspiration strikes, you'll have the resources to recognise it and act on it like McCartney and Dali.

Creative Takeaways

- Sleep deeply before you approach the blank page or the canvas.
- Remember, you must find it easy to begin your creative practise, and it should feel effective, efficient and rewarding (at least some of the time) if it's going to become a habit.

3

TRACE YOUR CREATIVE ROOTS

"The function of education is to teach one to think intensively and to think critically. Intelligence plus character – that is the goal of true education."
– Martin Luther King Jr.

Pay the bills, feed your family, exercise, meditate, paint, draw, play music, learn to cook, speak Spanish, travel to Peru, spend six months teaching English in Southeast Asia, record an album, craft artisanal clay pots, photograph your muse, study for an MBA, start a blog.

You could spend your life on thousands of worthwhile creative endeavours.

The painful realities of life complicate your ability to do what you want. And your options narrow the older you get.

If you want to become a more successful creative person, you will face tough decisions about what you'd like to do (like spending six months teaching English or travelling around Peru) and what you must do (compose an album, write a novel, etc).

Talent, opportunity and riches aren't enough. Talented artists might get off the starting blocks quicker than the rest of us, but their talents are of little use without an idea of where they're going.

The rich artist or the artist with more opportunities than his or her peers might be able to create flashier works than others (at least at first), but he or she will squander their talents or garb themselves in the "Emperor's New Clothes" unless they know what it's all for.

If you don't know where you're going, the current of life will sweep you along like an object afloat in a river, sometimes dashing you against the rocks and sometimes holding you back in a sluggish stream.

Your only real choice is to cast a rudder into the river, and while you're unable to control the current, you can at least steer your humble craft in the right direction.

Your Guiding Purpose

I once spent a year unemployed.

I was in a secure job that paid relatively well, but it was awful. When I couldn't stand the thought of staying even one more day, I broke from this job and found work as a press officer for a charity. It was supposed to be my dream job, but after several months my manager let me go.

He told me I didn't have what it takes. I contacted my old employer and asked for my job back, but I'd already burned the boats; there was no way I could return to my old and safe role.

I spent months out of work, considering what career I should follow. I knew I wanted to write, but I didn't know if this meant working in journalism, public relations or some other career.

I was adrift.

I eventually discovered people who are happy in their chosen professions face these types of crises armed with a personal mission statement, a guiding purpose or code.

They have done the hard work of educating themselves about what drives and inspires them. They know, too, that creativity doesn't just appear at will. It takes months and years of hard and purposeful work.

Originally from Chicago, singer and poet Patti Smith (b. 1946) has dedicated her life to the pursuit of art through poetry and punk rock. During the 1970s, she began performing poetry in clubs around New York and teaching herself how to play the guitar.

At first, Smith played alone in her room before performing for friends and then reciting poetry in small New York clubs.

Finally, she embraced the guitar and the microphone as her means of creative expression. After assembling her band, Patti knew at once they shared a guiding purpose. In *Just Kids*, she wrote:

 We imagined ourselves as the Sons of Liberty with a mission to preserve, protect, and project the revolutionary spirit of rock and roll . . .

We would call forth in our minds the image of Paul Revere, riding through the American night, petitioning the people to wake up, to take up arms. We too would take up arms, the arms of our generation, the electric guitar and the microphone."

Artists Henri Matisse (1869-1954) and Pablo Picasso (1881-1973) are two fine examples of artists with a guiding purpose.

Matisse worked solidly for 50 years at his craft. Even after abdominal cancer and a difficult operation left the elderly artist bedridden, he continued to create works of art in the form of paper cut-outs until his death.

Matisse found a *joie de vivre* in his art that wasn't possible anywhere else, and he famously said, "Work cures everything."

Picasso, sensing his mortality, used his art to look death in the eye. The last of his works tackle subjects like human sexuality, physical decay and his looming death. He also left instructions for anyone in search of creative success.

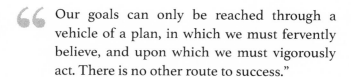

Our goals can only be reached through a vehicle of a plan, in which we must fervently believe, and upon which we must vigorously act. There is no other route to success."

Both artists paid attention to what drove them. Each figured out the purpose of their lives and pursued it to the end.

The Personal Mission Statement

Admit it.

You're afraid of spending so much time alone with ideas that might never pay off when you could be earning real money and experiencing more success in a regular job. You're afraid of the disapproving looks from your friends and family when you go into your room or studio alone, again.

You're scared of wasting your time, of making the wrong

decisions, of failing and, when you're honest with yourself, of not listening to the inner voice that whispers in the middle of the night, *create, damn it.*

Creative work involves so much ambiguity that you need a way of keeping motivated. You need a guiding purpose to navigate around your fears and explain, if only to yourself, why you do what you do.

No hard and fast rules ensure keeping motivated and figuring out what kind of creative person you are, but a personal mission statement will help.

A powerful support system, the personal mission statement will help you navigate the choppy currents of work and daily life.

When you face a big career decision, you'll be able to steer your craft in the right direction. You can use your mission statement to prevent being dashed upon the rocks or from getting stuck in shallow waters.

Now, you might be thinking a mission statement sounds like something a company or organisation would adopt, but in times of crisis or indecision, your personal mission statement will serve as your *oar.*

When I was unemployed, I used the exact process below to write my personal mission statement, find a way out of the darkness and decide what I was going to do with my career (or lack thereof).

Are you ready to get started?

Step 1: Map Your Life

Although you can do this at any time, a moment of crisis (like unemployment) is an ideal opportunity because you have the freedom to rethink every area of your life.

On a large piece of paper, map out the themes of your

life and work down from there. Typically, these include relationships, career, health, finances, education, family and religion. Expand on each theme to include your commitments, responsibilities and any work you've accomplished so far.

Finished? Great.

Next, consider the roles you play in your life. These might include being a spouse, parent, employer/employee, student, brother/sister and so on. Expand on each of these roles in terms of your aims, beliefs, principles, progress to date and causes of concern.

It's not necessary to go into detail; the point is to capture only what's important in your life and what you've achieved so far, to pay attention to what drives you and to what keeps you up at 3:00 a.m.

Step 2: Draw on External Resources

Next gather quotes, information and lessons from books you read, talks you attended, places you visited, music or art that inspires you or people you met.

Consider what inspires you and gets you out of bed in the morning, what you crave and what you would keep doing even if you won the lotto.

Look at the creative role models in your professional or personal life and consider what you can learn from them.

Read their biographies and examine what drives those you admire. See how they overcame personal and professional difficulties. Their lives should serve as a map that you can follow.

Spend time reading mission statements of others and see how they relate to your life. Undoubtedly your heroes took up many of the same roles and responsibilities that you now hold.

Journal writing is a great reflective practise for any creative professional, and if you keep one read through your older entries and look for a common theme or thread.

You should also consider organisations or people you *don't want to emulate* and determine how you can avoid making their mistakes. Remember, there's as much to learn from failure as from success.

Step 3: Ask Clarifying Questions

American mythologist and writer Joseph Campbell (1904-1987) famously told people to "follow your bliss" only to remark years later, that he should have said "Follow your blisters."

In other words, it's one thing to talk about following your passion, but you'll also need to take stock of what is causing you to struggle.

To do that, ask yourself searing questions about the themes of your life and each of your roles and areas of responsibility. Sample questions include:

- When am I at my best/worst as a parent/employer/ employee/spouse/artist etc.?
- Where do my natural talents lie?
- What's important to me in my work/home life?
- What energises me, and what makes me feel apathetic?
- What is my passion?
- Who inspires me in my work, relationships, etc.?
- Which role models can I emulate?

- What values guide my work/my studies/my relationships?
- Are there core values or principles I am not prepared to violate (these can include charters that you join)?
- How do these values relate to my day-to-day life?
- What mistakes have I made in my life so far, and how I can avoid repeating them?

You can write these questions down in a journal or expand on them using a mind map. If you're less visually oriented, you could write a personal question and answer document. Use bullet points or just record your thoughts using pen and paper.

Step 4: Consider the Wider Canvas

In the trenches of daily life, most people don't have time to think about where and who they'd like to become over the next 12 months, five or even ten years.

Now that you know better, include a wish list of places to visit, creative projects to accomplish, and dreams to realise.

Consider what you could create if you had unlimited time, money and resources.

Identify projects in each area of your life that will help you accomplish these dreams. Your list might include things like releasing a best-selling album or publishing a popular thriller series.

Don't just think big. Think IMAX!

After you're done with grandiosity, consider how your future creative project will impact other important areas of your life. What kind of compromises might you need to make? What kind of obstacles will you have to overcome?

For example, you might need to go back to college to study music and improve your skills, the trade-off being to give up some financial resources and time away from your family.

Can you balance your creative goals with your personal values? Nobody is going to answer this question for you.

Finally, remember to consider what happens *after* you accomplish a major life goal. Will the sacrifices it costs to paint a masterpiece be worth it and what will you do next?

Irish singer and artist Glen Hansard (b. 1970) has dedicated his entire life to creating music, but after he won an Oscar for writing the song "Falling Slowly", he fell into a depression and drank heavily. He figured out how to live with success only after meeting Bruce Springsteen.

 He said that everything I had ever been in my life – that guy struggling against the world – had died the night we won the Oscar. I was in a different part of my life, a different suit. He said I should learn to embrace it, enjoy it."

Step 5: Bring It All Together

You're almost there.

Gather your information into a single document or source. Then, consolidate your roles, areas of responsibility, values, goals and dreams into several principles. Start with statements like:

- "I believe ... "
- "I am happiest when ... "
- "I stand by ... "
- "I am at my best when ... "

If you're stuck, write a few lines about what you'd like people to say about your life at your ninetieth birthday party or your funeral. The final result could be a mantra or motto that you repeat or a longer piece of work that you read or review regularly.

You could try a mind map, picture, logo or even a simple sentence like the photographer Robert Mapplethorpe (1946-1989) who wanted to "live for art."

There's no right or wrong approach. Instead, what you're looking to do is document a simple system of beliefs or personal rules to live by (and in turn create).

Step 6: Put Your Mission Statement Into Practise

Congratulations!

By now, you should have a working personal mission statement, but you're probably wondering, what should I do with it?

You could hang your mission statement on your wall or keep it somewhere private but accessible, or you could put it in your drawer. Alternatively, you could expand on your personal mission statement and develop one for your family.

Once you've created your mission statement, start setting goals for your creative projects and take action to achieve what you want.

Then, when you know what to do, go and do it because nothing disappoints more than an artist who knows what they want to achieve but never gets started.

When trouble arrives, as it inevitably will, you'll be self-reliant and have an oar to guide you through choppy waters.

Of course, all of this activity is useless without reflection.

You don't want to spend years working on a creative project without occasionally asking yourself:

- "Is this worth doing?"
- "Am I living up to my personal beliefs?"
- "Do I know what's driving me?"

Put a few minutes aside once a month to review and update your mission statement and see if you're guiding your life in the right direction. You should have a system of personal beliefs that you refine as your life changes.

Work Beyond Chance and Fortune

You might be able to see the words in your head, have your colours arranged, a story at your fingertips or a muse for the camera, but you must act. Get the words out and your big ideas down.

Before you do, wait!

Pay attention to what's driving you. Decide what you want to achieve because, as the Stoic philosopher Lucius Seneca wrote, "When a man does not know what harbour he is making for, no wind is the right wind."

Now don't get me wrong, a personal mission statement is but one means of becoming unstuck and steering yourself towards the right harbour.

If it doesn't work for you, adopt a simple creed like the singer Patti Smith who lives for art or Pablo Picasso who had a creative plan he believed in until the very end.

A mission statement, a guiding purpose or even a simple artistic creed will help you sharpen your skills, develop your natural talents and spend your limited creative resources wisely.

Know that when you cast an oar into the river of life, you've already achieved more than those who are content to let chance and fortune carry them along.

My Personal Mission Statement

Below is my personal mission statement. When I showed this to a friend, he said he was impressed. I felt pleased with myself until he added, "You've a long way to go before you get there".

So take heart if yours feels ambitious. It doesn't have to look like mine. I've included mine as an example for you.

My mission is to pursue writing in all its forms and to create something from nothing. Writing is my shield and my sword, and this is how I will develop happiness.

I will teach my children how to become the kind of adults they were meant to be. I will demonstrate to them the virtues and challenges of temperance, love and patience. In doing so, I will foster these traits in myself.

I will seek physical and mental balance and avoid excess. I will avoid false and baseless pursuits and materialism because I know everything turns to ash. I will strive to reduce and refine rather than gather and accumulate.

I will practise empathy and conscientiousness. I will make sober decisions and embrace the idea of responsible risk-taking; that is I will live by Søren Kierkegaard's creed "To dare is to lose one's footing momentarily. Not to dare is to lose oneself."

I will lead a life of quiet integrity, for to speak ill of another is to damage myself. I will strive to understand the viewpoint of those I am against most. I will use moments of anger towards others as opportunities to learn more of my soul.

I will recognise my flaws, that I can become obsessive and impulsive, and I will seek to turn these flaws into virtues by becoming focused and brave. I will seek opportunities to practise kindness, temperance and patience because these are skills I must develop.

My time is finite. I will operate in my circle of influence rather than my circle of concern. I will put first things first. I will reflect upon the walls I am laying my ladders against.

I wither in stagnation, and I am energised when I am learning. I will burn myself completely like a good bonfire and leave no trace of myself behind (Shunryu Suzuki).

I will lean in.

Creative Takeaways

- Instead of letting life sweep you along, cast an oar into the river and guide yourself in the right direction.
- Do you have trouble making big decisions? Then, refer to your mission statement when you must make a decision as small as whether to practice when you don't feel like it or whether to invest in additional training.

4

LEARN WHAT YOUR CRAFT (AND YOUR AUDIENCE) DEMAND

"Begin challenging your assumptions. Your assumptions are the windows on the world. Scrub them off every once in awhile or the light won't come in."
– Alan Alda

I'm sitting at a large wooden table with my notepad and pen in front of me, a steaming cup of coffee beside me. I'm inside a warm, heated log cabin miles from the nearest village. I have food, heating, a laptop, a stack of unread books and a bold idea.

It's almost 09:00 a.m., but I don't have to get up from my desk, walk out into the cold, strap myself in my car and sit in traffic for an hour before I reach work.

In the cabin, there's a comfortable bed, a stocked fridge, a large wooden table and pictures of Thomas Edison and the choreographer Twyla Tharp on the wall to inspire me.

I'm miles from the nearest shop. When I open my

laptop, it doesn't ding or chime to notify me about emails, missed appointments and the demands of other people.

The mail carrier never calls. The phone doesn't ring. Here, alone in the woods, there is no one to keep happy, please or reassure.

I'm only interrupted when someone gently knocks on the door and leaves a breakfast of fresh fruit and strong coffee or a dinner of beef and Guinness stew sitting on the doorstep. I don't have to talk to anyone, thank anyone or apologise for what I'm doing.

Alone in the woods, I am finally free to work on my idea for hours at a time. I don't have to worry about what others think about me or my ideas.

And the problem with what I'm describing?

It's a fantasy.

Even if I could somehow find the time and resources to hole myself away in a creative retreat, there's little chance I'd finish something people would want to read in self-imposed solitude.

Would you?

Let me explain.

The idea of the lone artist toiling away in solitude, working on an idea for months or years at a time and then releasing a finished version of their work that succeeds is a falsehood.

I'm all for harnessing the power of solitude when you're at the start of a project, when you've no good ideas, when you want to practise your craft deliberately or become more comfortable with your work.

But, once you've given your idea form and substance you must expose it to the harsh light of critical, real-world feedback. You must test your underlying assumptions; see if your audience wants what you created. You must come out of the woods.

It's the only way to learn what your craft and your audience demand.

Pass the Salt

American businessman and inventor Thomas Edison (1847-1931) came up with thousands of inventions during his lifetime including the light bulb, a battery for an electric car and the motion picture camera.

A creative master, Edison challenged the assumptions of others – especially when he wanted to work with them.

When Edison met a potential employee, he tested the person's intelligence by asking a series of trivia questions like, "Where do we get prunes from?" or "Who invented printing?" and "What is felt?"

It was the early twentieth century after all.

Before offering a job, Edison took the applicant out for dinner and gave them a bowl of soup to eat. Then, Edison watched carefully to see what the job candidate did next.

If the unsuspecting candidate seasoned the soup with salt before tasting it, Edison didn't extend a job offer. On the other hand, if the candidate tasted the soup before seasoning it, Edison hired them.

He believed candidates who seasoned the soup without finding out if it needed salt was already full of unhelpful assumptions. This kind of person was of no use to Edison. He wanted to work with knowledgeable people who weren't full of preconceived ideas.

After all, this was a man who said, "Just because something doesn't do what you planned it to do doesn't mean it's useless."

Today, finding the origins of the prune is a Wikipedia search away. If you put the work in, read the right books and listen to the experts, you can school yourself on what you need to know about a topic or area of interest.

But the fundamentals of Edison's other test for job candidates remains: How can you challenge your assumptions?

Well, I'll be honest.

It's bloody hard to do it alone or if you're holed away in the woods.

I'd like to think if I reached Edison's shortlist, I'd sample his creamy vegetable soup before asking the waiter for the salt and pepper, but I'm an ordinary person with ordinary baggage and assumptions about how things should be.

I'd probably ask for the salt first.

Would you do the same?

Be honest.

If you're the kind of person who reaches for the metaphorical salt before tasting the soup, take a lesson from creative masters in the world of software development.

They are masters at challenging their assumptions, and they don't do it alone.

Learn What Your Audience Wants

Developing new software is an expensive and time-consuming business. The creative brains behind many of the tools and software programmes we use every day didn't get there by spending years of their lives and millions of dollars creating things people don't want.

Instead, many entrepreneurs turn their idea into a minimum viable product so they can challenge their assumptions and see if their customers want it *before* spending a significant amount of time or money on an idea.

Eric Reis (b. 1978) is an IT entrepreneur and author who popularised the concept of the minimum viable product. He explains:

 It's a version of a new product which allows a team to collect the maximum amount of validated learning about customers with the least effort."

Dropbox is an example of a successful minimum viable product.

Many great ideas are born because somebody had a problem they wanted to solve. Founder Drew Houston (b. 1983) came up with his idea for an easy-to-use file-sharing app because he was a forgetful MIT student.

He often left his USB behind, and every time he tried to share files with himself and others, he found technology was slow, buggy or difficult to use.

 I worked on multiple desktops and a laptop, and could never remember to keep my USB drive with me. I was drowning in email attachments trying to share files for my previous startup. My home desktop power supply literally exploded one day, killing one of my hard drives, and I had no backups."

Instead of reaching for the salt first and assuming his audience wanted his ideas, Houston developed an early concept. Then he created and narrated a three-minute video demonstrating the benefits of this easy-to-use file sharing service.

Houston packed his video with pop-culture Easter eggs and humorous references that resonated with the target audience of early adopters in the technology industry. At the end of the video, he asked viewers to register their interest by visiting the product's website.

Houston later said about his minimum viable product:

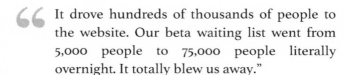 It drove hundreds of thousands of people to the website. Our beta waiting list went from 5,000 people to 75,000 people literally overnight. It totally blew us away."

After watching the rapid growth of this waiting list, Houston knew his underlying assumptions were right. People wanted an easy-to-use file-sharing service that worked. And he had proof.

From there, Houston and his team avoided wasting time and resources on things like mainstream PR and developing features that beta users didn't want.

Instead, they built a simple product that worked and people wanted. Then they were able to acquire money and resources to turn their minimum viable product into something they could sell.

You might not be concerned with software or products, but nothing is more dispiriting than creating something no one wants. Wasting time, money and your creative energy hurts.

So, how can you find out what your audience wants instead of relying on assumptions?

Remember intuition is helpful, but knowing your idea works is better. So, get an early version or minimum viable product of your idea in front of your would-be audience or peers.

Ask them for constructive feedback that you can use to improve and expand upon your original idea.

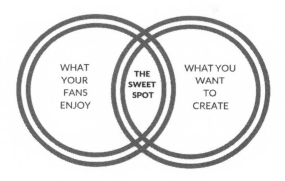

Find the sweet spot between what you create and what your fans will pay for

If you're a writer, release early chapters of your book to early or beta readers who provide you with feedback on how you can improve your work. Then, ask them if they'll pre-order your book so you have the financial resources to finish it.

Writer Hugh Howie (b. 1975), for example, didn't write all of his epic science-fiction series *Silo* in one go before releasing it. He wrote novella after novella and released each one separately because he recognised a demand for his ideas.

Others demonstrated their enthusiasm for his stories by opening their wallets.

If you're a musician, release some of your songs on social media or play them for people who aren't friends or family. Bands on tour often try out new and reworked songs in front of smaller audiences to see what works and what doesn't.

Bob Dylan (b. 1941) continually explores what his audience wants and likes. He constantly changes and rearranges his classic songs, sometimes to his audience's consternation and sometimes to their delight. He says,

 Getting an audience is hard. Sustaining an audience is hard. It demands a consistency of thought, of purpose, and of action over a long period of time."

If you're a painter, show an inner group of peers what you're working on, and use what they tell you to improve your work. Hell, even artists like Matisse and Picasso had patrons who supported their work financially *before* it was complete.

Your audience could love your idea; they could offer some harsh critical feedback or they could tell you it's terrible.

You could benefit from these opinions before you go any further. You don't want to spend months or years working on an idea only to find a big issue that's going to take months to fix or – worse – you've created something nobody wants.

After you've tested your minimum viable idea, you can do one of two things: Use your audience's critical feedback to improve your work or abandon your idea altogether and create something new.

Do you see what I'm saying? Good. Now that you know what your audience wants, let's cover . . .

Learn What Your Craft Demands

As a boy, Josh Waitzkin (b. 1976) was an American chess prodigy. He had an undeniable natural talent for the game, but what set him apart was how he learnt to play.

Waitzkin's coach Bruce Pandolfini presented Waitzkin with a barren chessboard and showed him how to play simple positions like king and pawn against a king. Once Waitzkin mastered these basic set pieces, Pandolfini added more pieces and built Waitzkin's knowledge incrementally. Waitzkin wrote:

> I was also gradually internalising a marvellous methodology of learning – the play between knowledge, intuition, and creativity. From both educational and technical perspectives, I learned from the foundation up."

Over the years and under the study of a few coaches, Waitzkin developed his knowledge of chess layer-by-layer, piece-by-piece and position-by-position. His peers, on the other hand, concentrated on learning complicated opening moves, assuming these short-term tactics would be enough to win any game.

> It's a little like developing the habit of stealing the test from your teacher's desk instead of learning to do the math. You may pass the test, but you learn absolutely nothing and most

critically, you don't gain an appreciation for
the value of learning itself."

As a competitor, Waitzkin faced a difficult problem.
Loops from popular music songs, whispering spectators and
the sound of a ticking clock kept getting stuck in his head
while he was trying to concentrate. At first, this threw Waitzkin off his game, but he couldn't do anything about it.

He realised his craft demanded an ability to concentrate
in an un-ideal environment. So, Waitzkin practised playing
chess at home with music playing full-volume and gradu-
ally adjusted to the noise of a busy tournament.

Waitzkin went on to become a champion chess player,
and he became an international master when he was 16.

Although he didn't have a minimum viable version of
his ideas to test, this prodigy succeeded at chess partly
because he used setbacks and victories as learning opportunities and to explore what his craft demanded.

Waitzkin is a creative master in more than chess. In his
early twenties, he began studying the martial art Tai
Chi Push.

To master this new art form, Waitzkin applied the same
incremental approach to learning that he'd cultivated as a
boy. It helped that years of competitive chess had already
given him the mental discipline required to master a sport
like Tai Chi.

Waitzkin rose quickly through the ranks of Tai Chi Push
Hands and became a national champion in the United
States.

In 2000, he competed in his first Push Hands World
Championships in Taiwan. Waitzkin assumed the World
Championships would be similar to the American compe-
titions, but instead he found himself in an alien environ-

ment where no one spoke English or told him what was going on.

During the competition, the U.S. champion waited for his match for hours, getting hungry and anxious. Eventually, he ate a greasy pork lunch. Immediately afterwards, the announcer called his name to begin competing.

"I got destroyed," Waitzkin wrote about that match. "It wasn't even close."

After reflecting on his disappointing tournament, Waitzkin realised he wasn't prepared for the mental and physical demands of international competition.

Over the next few years, the former chess champion focused on his physical form and his mental attitude. He taught himself how to overcome setbacks like a last-minute change to the rules. Waitzkin even deliberately practised competing against a training partner, Frank, who didn't play by the rules.

Frank liked to jab his hand into Waitzkin's Adam's apple if he was about to lose a match.

"I quickly realised that the reason I got angry when he went after my neck was that I was scared," wrote Waitzkin. "There will always be creeps in the world, and I had to learn how to deal with them with a cool head."

Waitzkin competed again in 2002, and in 2004 he became a world champion title holder.

Although you might not be squaring off against a martial art competitor, your creative work still demands you learn new skills and hone existing ones like Waitzkin did.

Perhaps you need to teach yourself how to keep going when you feel like quitting. Or maybe learning to sit quietly in a room and paint or draw for two hours at a time without being distracted is your private victory.

Several years ago, I started tracking how long I spent

writing, what I wrote and my daily word count in a spreadsheet. I'm not a numbers person, but this self-quantification helped me see exactly how much I was able to create each day and whether I was working as hard as I imagined.

I was able to compare my completed stories and articles against my word count for each month and discover when I was most and least creative. I also began writing down lessons about storytelling, writing, creativity and more so I could apply what I'd come across in my work.

Consider how you can track your creative output and start documenting lessons you've learnt about your craft in a journal or notebook.

If you're new, this kind of insight is invaluable because your peers, friends and family either won't understand or care about the strides you're making in your work.

They can see only the external output, the finished stories, the released music tracks, the photo collections and so on. Your audience has no way of measuring your growth as an artist or celebrating that you've learnt to deal with issues like fear and self-doubt.

In the end, you must mark these learning milestones, lest you forget them.

Create Alone and in Company

Learning what your craft or your audience demands is an art form.

When you're first acquiring a creative skill, start with the fundamentals. Although you won't have much to show for your hard work at first, build privately on each of your hard-earned lessons over time. Keep track of your progress so at least you can see how much you've come on and avoid reaching for the salt first.

As you become more accomplished at your chosen craft, don't give up on learning more of what your craft demands.

Like the meditator who discovers the intricacies of his or her breath by focusing on it each day, your work will reveal more to you over the weeks, months and years.

It's a lifelong practise, and it's one that separates the amateur from the professional and the professional from the creative master.

Consider what your audience wants too. When you're ready, show them a minimum viable idea and ask for critical feedback and if they're prepared to support you. Then, use their critical feedback or financial backing to improve your craft or ideas.

Of course, sometimes you don't need to worry about having a minimum viable idea.

If you're pursuing a passion project or a private creative work, by all means, do what you will. Or if your focus is an abstract project that you believe is pushing your chosen discipline forwards, then don't concern yourself with what others want.

History is full of instances when an inspired artist gave his or her audience something so shocking or original that they didn't know how to react. When Wolfgang Amadeus Mozart first released his music, his peers and audience lamented his composition was too rich in ideas, artful and difficult to understand.

Today, we could call these people Philistines but those moments are rare!

Remember, though, unless you've bought into the myth of the lone, starving artist, getting a minimum viable product or idea will help you test your assumptions and avoid wasting your limited time and creative energy.

The effort will help you learn more about your craft, faster.

So unless you're happy to create alone and in obscurity, trace the connection between what your audience wants and what you've created.

When you see a divide, bridge it.

Creative Takeaways

- Come out of your bat cave, go and meet your audience and show them what you've got. Study their reactions intensely.
- Start tracking your progress and what you've learnt about your craft.

5

FIND A CREATIVE MASTER

"No one is really going to help you or give you direction. In fact, the odds are against you."
– Robert Greene

Stop it.

Stop feeling sorry for yourself.

You might think your problems are special, unique, or impossible for anyone else to understand. But you know what?

We're all struggling with the same basic creative problems.

You're not the only one who struggles, wants to think outside the box, needs motivation to keep going or craves critical feedback about their work.

You're not the only one who spends hours tinkering with your ideas and still hates them. And you're not the only one who'll do anything–clean the bathroom, service the car, run a marathon–to avoid sitting your ass in the chair and doing the work.

Almost every creative person faces problems like procrastination, perfectionism and self-doubt at one time or another. Even the successful ones.

But the feeling of being utterly alone on your artist's journey is insidious. It gnaws at your confidence and weakens your resolve. It causes talented writers to give up when all they need to do is keep going. And that needs to stop right now.

Your Map

Imagine the scene.

You're driving along a deserted road.

You haven't seen another car, another person or even a road sign in hours. The car's old engine has been making a strange rattling sound since you left home, and each time you hit another pothole, you think the engine might drop right out.

Regardless, you push your fears aside, sit up straight in your seat, and keep driving. Because while your destination is not on any map, others have told you it's worth the journey. But it'll be dark soon, and the fuel gauge is straying dangerously close to empty.

A while back, when my fuel gauge was close to empty, I came across advice from the recently departed American historical author E.L. Doctorow (1931-2015). He once said,

 Writing is like driving at night in the fog. You can only see as far as your headlights, but you can make the whole trip that way."

It's a powerful metaphor and one you can apply to playing music, painting, drawing or most kinds of creative work. But if you're anything like me, you hate feeling lost.

You can't stand the sense that you might be on the wrong track, leaving a trail of wasted time and effort. Like anyone who works with ideas, I long for road markings or helpful directions from someone who has completed the same journey before me.

Seek Help from Past Masters

The mentor/student relationship is an age-old one.

By the thirteenth century, a young person in Western Europe who aspired to become a blacksmith, carpenter or even an artist served an apprenticeship. He or she worked for a master craftsman from age 15 onwards in exchange for food, board and instruction.

An apprenticeship lasted about seven years and, once complete, the young person could work as a journeyman or day labourer for wages.

Apprentices who aspired to become masters had to create a great work approved by the town guild and pay the group a hefty fee. As a master, they could take on apprentices and teach their skills.

Apprenticeships were expensive and sought after, and many of them never acquired a workshop of their own or became masters.

Today, having a mentor offers opportunities to learn a creative skill faster and gain access to the creative insight and resources of those who have gone before you.

Many modern-day creative masters sought the help of mentors to guide their careers.

For example, American writer Stephen King (b. 1947)

attributes the success of his many books to his wife Tabby, who is also a writer. He shows Tabby early drafts of his books and asks her about tone, what he should put in and take out.

King counts on her as the one person who will say that he's working too hard or that he should slow down. It was Tabby who picked an earlier version of his first novel *Carrie* that agents rejected out from the wastepaper basket. She told a young and disillusioned King there was something in his story. He wrote,

 [Tabby] wanted me to go on with it . . . She wanted to know the rest of the story . . . 'You've got something here,' she said. 'I really think you do.'"

An ideal creative mentor takes more than a passing interest in your work. These mentors want you to grow and develop as a creative person, and they will instruct you in their chosen art.

A mentor will show you how to avoid committing common mistakes and help you learn the skills of your creative trade faster. They will expose you to higher levels of creative thinking and provide you with critical feedback beyond what your friends, family, readers, listeners or critics offer.

You will become more accomplished and creative if you have a mentor to guide you, but *how can you find a mentor* and *what should you do once you've found one*?

Distinguish Between Good and Great Mentors

I spent my twenties trying and failing to earn a living as a successful Irish journalist. I would have given almost anything for a more experienced journalist to take an interest in the course of my career and show me what to do and what to avoid.

I was prepared to strike a Faustian pact, if you will.

Several of my classmates from journalism college worked with editors and more experienced colleagues who took an interest in their careers, but I always found it difficult to settle in a newspaper or radio station.

I grew resentful and was happy to tell people outside of the profession that most journalists were unhelpful.

I'd failed to see the big problem behind my petty resentments. During a career, people have many kinds of mentors. There are good mentors and great mentors; the former is easy to acquire while the latter is an elusive prize.

Good mentors are the teachers and instructors in your local creative writing, music or film class. They are respected colleagues in the workplace or even some of your friends.

Even more importantly, they can help you advance your creative career faster, even if you work with or follow that mentor for just a little while.

The good news is it's relatively easy to find a good mentor. A more experienced colleague that you can trust can serve this role for a time (although you might not want to label the relationship) or you can hire a teacher or instructor to work directly with you.

Great mentors are fewer and farther between and harder to find. They are creative masters whose work keeps you up at night because it's so damn good.

So how can you find a great mentor?

If that person is still living and working, figure out how you could be useful to them. Try to look at the world through the gaze of your mentor, asking yourself, "What does he or she need most?"

Transform yourself into someone with skills that complement their work.

Yes, this means you're going to have to work for free. I know giving away your time for nothing is troubling, but I'd like to reframe what you're doing as a trade: Your time for access to their expertise.

Great mentors almost always complain about a lack of free time. One great way to hook their attention is to do something that gives your would-be mentor more hours to spend. If you're a writer, for example, you could offer to write an article or a blog post for their website.

You can also work with great mentors as part of a group.

Let's say you are a musician.

You and several of your peers could sign up for a workshop or retreat with a talented musician during which your mentor provides you and the rest of the group critical feedback over a couple of days.

You can also short-circuit this process if you're prepared to either pay a great mentor for one-on-one feedback or if you shift your definition of the student/mentor relationship.

Your Council of Mentors

What I'm going to tell you next makes me sound crazy.

I talk to dead people.

No, I'm not referring to ghosts or strangers who haunt my house. I talk to American novelist and short story writer John Cheever (1912-1982).

Known as the "Chekhov of the suburbs," he wrote five novels and a number of short story collections during his creative career. Six weeks before his death, Cheever was awarded the National Medal for Literature by the American Academy of Arts and Letters.

He died in 1982 when I was only a year old.

So if I never met Cheever and he died when I was a baby, how can he be one of my creative mentors?

Several years ago, I read *The Journals of John Cheever*, a book that gave me insight into his creative process. Then I read several of Cheever's novels, as well as books by writers who influenced him.

Tracing the roots of his big ideas helped me understand why Cheever made some of his creative choices and gave me more of a feeling for what inspired him as a writer.

For a long time afterwards, when faced with a creative challenge I visualised Cheever and asked him, "What would you do?" Now, his manifesto guides me.

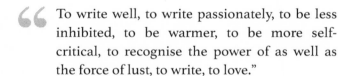 To write well, to write passionately, to be less inhibited, to be warmer, to be more self-critical, to recognise the power of as well as the force of lust, to write, to love."

I'm aware this makes me sound quite mad, but it's a creative process that American author Napoleon Hill (1883-1970) recommended in his seminal book *Think and Grow Rich!*

He suggested keeping an "imaginary council" every night that you consult when you have a problem or need advice.

He wrote,

Just before going to sleep at night, I would shut my eyes, and see, in my imagination, this group of men seated with me around my Council Table.

I had a very definite purpose in indulging my imagination through these nightly meetings. My purpose was to rebuild my own character so it would represent a composite of the characters of my imaginary counsellors."

Hill's council comprised nine of his mentors including Thomas Edison and Charles Darwin–people Hill never met. There's no psychological trickery behind his approach either.

Instead, push yourself to learn from every possible source that your imaginary mentor offers. Read the books they cite, listen to what inspired them and trace the roots of their creative work until you unearth their influences. Be rigorous about applying what your mentor has to teach.

Be Selective

What if you're working with a mentor who got lucky or one who doesn't know what they are doing? What if their teachings are stale and out of date? What if your values clash with theirs?

Before you select your creative mentor, research your needs and their qualities thoroughly.

To find out if a creative mentor is suitable, write a list of your weaknesses, needs and areas where you need improvement.

Perhaps you need help playing musical scales, adding texture to your paintings or weaving stories into your works.

Or maybe you're struggling to learn from each of your practise sessions. Or perhaps you need help with the tactics of your craft. And so on.

Find a mentor who is farther along the path you're walking or turn towards a mentor who has mastered one of your obvious deficiencies. They must be able to help you address the areas where you need help.

Read everything about your potential mentor and find critics of their work so you can assess whether the relationship will work. It's best to discover the potential flaws of your would-be mentor before you've invested a significant amount of time, money and creative resources following their path.

Once you spend money or time on a mentor, this sunken cost complicates turning away from their teachings, even if it's foolish to throw good money after bad.

When you are selecting a mentor, consider your psychology.

Ask honest questions about your tolerance for risk and failure.

Many creative masters take bold and dramatic risks on the path towards success and fail hard before they achieve their goals.

Stephen King's novel *Carrie* was rejected 30 times before his wife fished it out of the bin. Walt Disney was a creative visionary, but he spent much of his career teetering on the brink of bankruptcy and even voiced contempt for the financial backers who helped him out.

J.K. Rowling wrote the first Harry Potter book while jobless, divorced and raising a child alone.

Do you have the stomach for these kinds of risks and failures?

A great mentor doesn't have to become your friend, but

you must be able to listen to them without feeling irritated or despondent. Consider how you will react to their beliefs, leadership style, way of thinking, systems, mannerisms, speech and ideals.

Remember, a great mentor will help you connect ideas in exciting ways, think on a higher level and achieve your creative goals faster. Choose well!

Burn Your Mentor's Ideas Into Your Own

Read, watch and listen to everything your mentor sends you, produces or creates. Keep a file or a notebook and write down everything they have to teach you and review regularly what you've learnt from them.

Whenever you face a decision about how to spend your time or resources, use your mentor's teachings to guide you. Ask them questions and, if possible get them to review your work and provide critical feedback.

Do what they tell you, and put as much of their teachings into practise as you can at the expense of advice you hear elsewhere. The fire of your mentor's teachings should temper you so that you can face external ideas and challenges without becoming overwhelmed.

At first, your mentor's advice might seem odd and even against your better instincts, but remember your mentor knows far more about the creative journey you're both on.

Later, when you start to achieve results, you can bring more of your experiences and knowledge into your chosen creative field.

Nothing lasts forever.

There will come a point when you must develop self-reliance and strike out on your own. It will naturally arrive if you've hired a mentor to work with you for a pre-determined period or if they're working with you in a more distanced capacity. Be sure you're both prepared to make the break.

If you are working directly with your mentor and have hooked their attention, they might become dependent on you and even hold you back.

They might want to keep you within the fold because they need you or even because they are afraid you will outshine them.

If this happens, remember the goal of any mentoring relationship isn't life-long friendship; your creative work must come first.

Prepare for the Journey Ahead

The road at the beginning of any creative journey appears long and mysterious. Realising you've got only a vague idea of where you're going or wondering if you're going to reach your destination soon is never pleasant.

Yes, the look of *your* journey will be different from the next person's, but make no mistake: You are not the first person to embark on this creative path.

Many others are willing to show you the way if you have the guts to ask. Follow the path that writers, artists, painters, filmmakers and creative masters have walked before you. The next time you encounter a creative problem, ask yourself what would your mentor do.

As you become more skilled at your craft, start questioning some of your mentor's ideas and teachings.

Challenge your mentor.

They might not like this pushback, and many mentor/student relationships end acrimoniously. However, if you go into this type of relationship with your eyes open, you will be prepared for the inevitable end of the mentor/student relationship.

When you reach this crossroad, look for another, better mentor to guide you.

Say to yourself: *Onwards!*

You can draw on the strengths of one mentor to offset the weaknesses of the next. It's why writers work with more than one editor during their career, and it's why musicians move from one producer to the next.

By tapping into the knowledge of multiple experts, you will fashion yourself into a creative person other people seek out.

By going from one creative mentor to the next, you will combine the teachings of various teachers with your unique ideas and creative voice.

This combination of the accomplished and the new will help you grow into an exciting and fresh creative talent.

You just have to be brave enough to keep going.

Creative Takeaways

- Write down a hit list of people you would like to have as your creative mentor. Remember, they can be alive, dead, accessible or inaccessible.
- Next time you face a creative challenge, visualise your mentor and ask what would they do.

6

STRENGTHEN YOUR MIND AND YOUR BODY

"Pain is inevitable. Suffering is optional."
– Haruki Murakami

"Things aren't going well here for you Bryan," my boss said.

I was working as a press officer for a charity. It was supposed to be my dream job. You know the kind: Earn an honest wage, work nine-to-five hours, drink nice coffee and tell myself I'm finally making a difference in the world.

I was all for it, and this was my first performance review.

"Are you listening, Bryan?" my boss asked. "You missed an important deadline; you caused confusion for other members of your team, and there were mistakes in your work."

On a Wednesday morning in November, we were sitting in a quiet room away from the hum of the office.

"There's so much to learn," I said.

I accepted I was guilty of mistakes, of incompetence. I

produced an important report with typos, a presentation with incorrect slides and I'd missed a meeting with a client.

"I'm sorry. I can do better, just give me more time."

He adjusted narrow-frame silver glasses. "You've got three months, but you need to put that master's you studied for into action."

"I'll try," I said. "I'll do better."

That night, I bought a popular book about productivity and implemented every strategy I could understand. I reread my boss's emails, searching for actions I'd missed.

I sent the management team weekly updates of my accomplishments. I even pinned a quote from Viktor E. Frankl's *Man's Search For Meaning* to the wall near my desk.

> Live as if you were living already for the second time and as if you had acted the first time as wrongly as you are about to act now."

I embraced the job, but no matter what I did I couldn't figure out how to give my boss (and his boss) what they needed. Every project I worked on failed. I tried to send e-Christmas cards to the charity's mailing list only to find I'd compiled a list of the wrong recipients.

I created a development plan for the charity's website that my boss didn't want to read, and I wrote a 2,000-word profile of the organisation's work that the management team said they couldn't publish.

I felt as if I were under attack.

After Christmas, my boss called me back into that room.

"We're letting you go, Bryan. The work you're doing here isn't much beyond that of a clerical officer in the civil service, and that's not what this charity needs." My boss slid a white envelope across the table. "Here's your notice."

I felt like taking the envelope, ripping it up and throwing it at him. Not even Viktor Frankl could help me.

"I left a good job to come here." I thought of the permanent and pensionable job I'd had as care worker for people with intellectual disabilities.

"What am I supposed to do now?" I asked.

"This is hard for me," he said. "I know it must be hard for you."

I folded the envelope in two.

How could this be hard for him when I was the one losing a job in the middle of a recession with my wife and two small children depending on me?

"When do I finish?"

He folded his hands.

"We'll give you till the end of February alongside whatever holiday pay you're due."

I left the room and walked out the front door and into the small car park. I got into my rusting 2002 Renault Clio. Then I punched the ceiling over and over and swore as loudly as I could get away with in a business park at 3:00 p.m. on a grey Monday afternoon in January.

For weeks afterwards, I was angry about being fired, being out of a job and claiming social welfare. I tried to write about it, but I didn't make much progress.

I couldn't find a way to balance my anger and disappointment with the calmness writing demands, and the endurance I needed to look for another job.

I looked outwards toward the biographies of artists I admired for answers. I wanted to see how they overcame personal and professional setbacks and still found strength to work on their ideas.

What I found surprised me. Some of these creative

masters lived deeply unhappy lives, while others knew how
to change their destructive habits for the better.

The Drunken Miserable Artist

Do you believe alcohol or drugs unlocks fresh thinking that
sobriety can't? Are you prepared to sacrifice present or
future happiness for more inspired ways of thinking?

A pernicious myth suggests the best artists are unapolo-
getic drug addicts and alcoholics. They take pride in being
tortured souls who tap into a higher creative power. They
can only support their immense talents with the crutch of
alcohol and drugs.

Yes, alcohol and drugs will help you view the world
differently and even come up with original ideas . . . at least
at first.

Neuroscientist and philosopher Sam Harris (b. 1967)
consumed psychedelic drugs such as LSD and magic mush-
rooms in his early twenties as part of his search for new
ideas about the universe and himself. However, Harris
likens his approach to strapping himself to a rocket ship.

 If LSD is like being strapped to a rocket,
learning to meditate is like gently raising a
sail. Yes, it is possible, even with guidance, to
wind up someplace terrifying, and some
people probably shouldn't spend long periods
in intensive practise. But the general effect of
meditation training is of settling ever more
fully into one's own skin and suffering
less there."

Artists like William Faulkner, Ernest Hemingway, John

Cheever, John Berryman, Raymond Carver, F. Scott Fitzgerald, Amy Winehouse, Vincent Van Gogh, Yoko Ono, and Neil Young were compelled to strap themselves to their personal rocket ships, but look closer and you'll see that these artists also recognised the value of sobriety.

Take Ernest Hemingway (1899-1961). He was a prolific and inspired writer, but he was also notorious for drinking heavily. His biographer Anthony Burgess wrote:

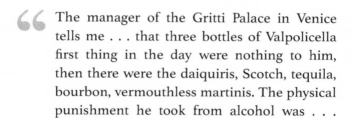

> The manager of the Gritti Palace in Venice tells me . . . that three bottles of Valpolicella first thing in the day were nothing to him, then there were the daiquiris, Scotch, tequila, bourbon, vermouthless martinis. The physical punishment he took from alcohol was . . . actively courted."

Although he struggled with alcoholism, Hemingway went to great lengths to sober up before the end his life, and he never wrote while drunk. In *Interview Magazine*, Hemingway's granddaughter, Mariel, said about him,

> That's not how he wrote. He never wrote drunk, he never wrote beyond early, early morning . . . So many writers glorify my grandfather's way of living as much as they glorify his work. And so they try and mirror that. I think it's the misperception of addiction and living life on the edge, as if it's cool."

Hemingway struggled until the very end.

On Saturday the 2nd of July 1961, Hemingway rose early, unlocked the storage room of his house in Ketchum, Idaho, and took out a shotgun he used for shooting pigeons. Hemingway walked to the foyer of his house, put the twin barrels against this forehead, and pressed the trigger.

The American poet John Berryman (1914-72) relied on drink to stabilise him and offset the startling intensity he brought to his poetry. He got into drunken arguments with his landlord, was arrested, fell, suffered hallucinations, was hospitalised, gave public lectures that he couldn't remember and was divorced three times.

While in treatment in 1970, he wrote,

"Wet bed drunk in a London hotel, manager furious, had to pay for a new mattress, $100. Lectured too weak to stand, had to sit. Lectured badly prepared. Too ill to give an examination, colleague gave it. Too ill to lecture one day. Literary work stalled for months. Quart of whiskey a day for months. Wife desperate, threatened to leave unless I stopped. Two doctors drove me to Hazelden last November, 1 week intensive care unit, 5 wks treatment. AA 3 times, bored, made no friends. First drink at Newlbars' party. Two months light drinking, hard biographical work. Suddenly began new poems 9 weeks ago, heavier & heavier drinking more & more, up to a quart a day. Defecated uncontrollably in university corridor, got home unnoticed. Book finished in outburst of five weeks, most intense work in my whole life exc. maybe first two weeks of 1953."

While reading that, my heart went out to Berryman's suffering, to a man who never found an answer to his problems. On Friday, January 7, 1972, he got the bus to Washington Avenue Bridge, climbed onto the railing, fell 100 feet, missed the Mississippi River and landed on a nearby embankment.

Short story writer and poet Raymond Carver (1938-1988) struggled with alcohol for years, too.

In late 1977, he went to a dinner party with friends, drank a glass of wine and blacked out. The next thing he remembered was standing outside a store the following morning waiting for it to open so he could buy a bottle of vodka. Then he attended a meeting with an editor who wanted to buy his book; Carver was both drunk and hungover.

It was enough of a low for Carver to finally find a better way to live with his pain. He told the *Paris Review* about his decision to quit drinking,

> I stayed drunk for a couple more days. And then I woke up, feeling terrible, but I didn't drink anything that morning. Nothing alcoholic, I mean. I felt terrible physically--mentally, too, of course--but I didn't drink anything. I didn't drink for three days, and when the third day had passed, I began to feel some better. Then I just kept not drinking. Gradually I began to put a little distance between myself and the booze. A week. Two weeks. Suddenly it was a month. I'd been sober for a month, and I was slowly starting to get well."

After he stopped drinking, Carver enjoyed 10 good and creative years before dying of cancer at age 50. In the poem "Gravy" – which is inscribed on his grave – he wrote:

> *"Don't weep for me,"*
> *he said to his friends. "I'm a lucky man.*
> *I've had ten years longer than I or anyone*

expected. Pure Gravy. And don't forget it."

Ten years doesn't seem like much, but Carver used these years to give his creative work the respect and attention it demanded, and unlike some of his peers, he found a measure of happiness.

The stories of these creative masters demonstrates that creativity demands clear, level-headedness, and that pure gravy will come only if you're healthy and strong.

The Unbreakable Link Between Mind and Body

So, you want to become the kind of artist who has the energy to turn up every day in front of the blank page and create. You're looking for a way of focusing on your big idea without getting distracted, and you'd like to finish what you're working on without sacrificing your happiness.

If only there were something that would help you do all this . . . without strapping yourself to a rocket ship.

There is.

For me, the best, most creative days come when I run and meditate. Meditation and exercise will help you embrace positive change in many different ways. Many productive artists pursue activities like these.

I've spent some tough times here.

Focus on Your Big Ideas

Meditation is scientifically proven to aid concentration, improve our memory and make us smarter. Those who meditate for 20 minutes or more thrice a week are better able to focus on a task and less prone to mood swings.

Running is a lot like meditation.

Think about it:

Both meditation and running demand that you turn up several times a week on your cushion or in your trainers and commit to one difficult task for an extended period.

Both activities involve focusing on the breath at length, just as aspiring artists must learn to concentrate on the ideas before them.

The runner knows one bad training session doesn't mean they are unfit or unprepared for a race. The next day, they simply put their trainers back on and keep going.

The meditator acknowledges day-to-day setbacks alongside small accomplishments, accepting both as they move forward.

If you're an artist who exercises intensely (or meditates),

a short story, painting or a complicated piece can feel more achievable. You can take the lessons learnt on the track or the cushion and break down a big idea into a series of small milestones.

Then you can focus on achieving small personal victories, overcoming minor setbacks and slowly progressing towards your goal.

Give Your Monkey Mind a Break

If you're a desk monkey like me, you spend up to eight hours a day looking at a screen, in your office on your phone, and in front of the television.

Like me, you might look at your bloodshot eyes in the mirror and wonder if all this screen time is rotting your brain, killing your concentration and making you go blind.

Your body and mind crave a break from the glare of screens, monitors and devices.

Give them what they want.

Then when you sit down to work on your creative project, you will be able to see the hook for your article, the typo on page two and the plot twist that your tired, overworked mind missed an hour ago.

Transform into a More Productive Artist

As a writer, I'm fascinated by how artists get things done. Here's what I discovered:

Most creative masters are nothing like Ernest Hemingway or John Berryman. They aren't alcoholics; they are disciplined, sober and health-conscious. Also, Hemingway and Berryman both tried to sober up towards the end.

Take Haruki Murakami (b. 1949). He is one of Japan's greatest novelists and the author of books like *Kafka on the Shore* and *What I Talk About When I Talk About Running*. He's also a serious athlete who runs at least one marathon a year. When Murakami is writing a novel, he says he runs or swims for at least an hour a day.

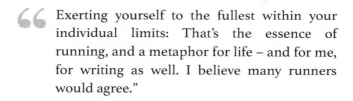

Exerting yourself to the fullest within your individual limits: That's the essence of running, and a metaphor for life – and for me, for writing as well. I believe many runners would agree."

When I'm in pain, I think of that sentence. I force myself to run a little farther, a little harder. Later, I try to write a while longer and go that bit deeper.

Fight Depression and Eliminate Stress

Steven Pressfield wrote in *Turning Pro* when the professional artist is in pain, he or she takes "two aspirin and keeps on trucking", but even he would agree it's easier to work on your ideas when you're not in pain.

The good news is intense physical exercise like running helps you lose weight, fight disease and sleep better, and when you are physically and mentally healthier, you are better able to concentrate on your ideas.

If good health isn't enough reason to run, anyone who trains several times a week experiences a runner's high, which I can vouch for. The natural feel-good endorphins that running releases carry over after you've finished, into your work.

When I run five or ten kilometres, the chair, my

computer, the keyboard, the blank screen, and the flashing cursor all become irresistible.

You might be thinking,

Stop, I hate running!

Swap running for any aerobic activity, and you'll get all the benefits listed above.

You can swim, cycle, box, golf, row, ski, dance, play tennis or squash, hike or even cut grass, and still become a more productive and creative writer.

Letting Go

I discovered meditation before being fired.

I first considered it a way to focus on work and become a model employee. But then I found myself without a job, and the intimidating red cushion demanded, "Sit!".

I refused to sit for weeks.

To sit and look inwards, to face my anxiety and disappointment when I should have been working and writing struck me as preposterous.

Damn that cushion!

One day I received a rejection for a new job I was perfect for. I brooded about it all day, and I argued with my wife about money that evening. Later that night, I tossed and turned in bed and considered who had wronged me.

At 3:00 a.m., I got up, went downstairs and sat on the large red cushion. I clasped my hands, took a deep breath and closed my eyes. I meditated on the faces of my family and thanked them for their support. I meditated on the faces of people I worked with, and I wished them well in their careers.

Finally, I meditated on the face of my boss. I could see his pale, lined face, his crisp white shirt and his dark wavy hair. My hands tightened, my foot began to ache, and a line of sweat ran down the small of my back.

"I forgive you for letting me go," I said.

I won't lie. Ten minutes of meditation didn't siphon all my anger, but it pierced a hole, and enough eased out that I could sleep.

Finding meaningful employment took another six months.

Several weeks into a new role in a profession I didn't expect, I thought of my old boss and the pressure he was under from his boss. In my journal, I wrote about how he didn't have to give me holiday pay or write me a good reference and of how he did all of those things.

Through the one thing I knew how to do before I was fired and the one thing I kept trying to do after I was fired – writing – I saw my mistakes for what they were and the role for what it was: One I wasn't built for. And it was OK.

I could learn to let go too.

Creative Takeaways

- Cultivate physical and mental strength and endurance so you can approach the blank page or virgin canvas without fear.
- Your pursuit of physical and mental strength and endurance should support your creative work, not the other way around.

7

INVEST IN YOUR SIDE PROJECTS

"A musician must make music, an artist must paint, a poet must write, if he is to be ultimately at peace with himself."
– Abraham Maslow

AFTER WRITING a lengthy charity grant application for several weeks, I was exhausted. When my boss at my main gig asked me to perform simple tasks, I tried not to snap at her.

When my friends asked how the new job was going and if I was still writing, I cracked cynical jokes about how it was a waste of time.

I didn't know it then, but I was burnt-out and unhappy.

Christina Maslach from The University of California Berkeley and Susan E. Jackson from NYU are authorities on this subject.

They said workers who are burnt-out "feel unhappy about themselves and dissatisfied with their accomplishments on the job."

I blame myself.

I should have listened to Abraham Maslow.

In 1943, this American psychologist explained individuals can be happy only if they can express themselves and achieve their potential. These were all things I wasn't doing.

If you're a musician, you must play, if you're a writer, you must get the words down, and if you're an artist, you must fill the virgin canvas.

Maslow called this "self-actualisation" and cautioned "the story of the human race is the story of men and women selling themselves short."

Don't sell yourself short.

If your main gig isn't giving you enough time or space to write, draw, paint or play, if you spend your nine-to-five responding to the demands of others, or if you work on projects only because they pay the bills, you need a side project.

Hell, even if you love your main gig, a side project will prevent you from becoming burnt-out, and it could put food on your table down the road.

Recognising Side Projects

When you're messing around and jamming, when it's just for kicks, when nobody gets hurt, gets paid or gets laid, it's a side project.

When you're working alone with an idea and an editor isn't screaming about deadlines, it's a side project.

When it's an idea for a TV show you carry on set every day and pull out when you've got a few free hours, it's a side project.

When it's a band you play with for fun after your main gig is done, it's a side project.

When you take pictures for hours at the weekend and

stay up late at night fretting about white balance and colour compositions, it's a side project.

When it's a haiku you write on the back of a white envelope in between boardroom meetings, it's a side project.

When you're bored and sitting on the train or waiting for a plane and you're doodling on the back of a beermat, it's a side project.

When you can't bring yourself to throw it away, it's a side project.

When you're stuck, blocked and procrastinating, when your main thing is the painful thing, it's a side project.

When you think you're messing around, and something unexpected happens, it's a side project.

When you knock your big ideas off each other like billiard balls, it's a side project.

When they produce an unexpected little idea, it's a side project.

When it's the fun you have when all the other work is done, it's your side project.

Just ask Matthew Weiner.

How Matthew Weiner Carved Out Time for His Side Project

Ever since he was a boy, Matthew Weiner (b. 1965) wanted to become a writer. He was born into a home in Baltimore that revered writers, but when Weiner attempted to follow in the footsteps of his creative heroes, he was rejected time and again.

He wrote poetry and stories and tried to join writing class after writing class. A professor who read some of Weiner's early poetry told him, "I think you know you are not a poet."

Weiner studied literature, philosophy and history at

Wesleyan University and attended film school at the University of Southern California.

After graduating, he stayed at home for three years and spent his time writing spec scripts for television shows.

While his friends got real, paying day jobs, Weiner struggled to break into show business as a writer. He relied on his wife, who was an architect, to support him.

Like many new artists, Weiner couldn't handle the constant rejection and lack of success. His main gig wasn't paying off. So he stopped writing and considered getting a real job that paid well with the rest of his friends.

Then, Weiner got a break that changed his life.

Through an old college friend, Weiner found his first paying job as a television writer for a pilot that needed a polish or a "punch-up".

Weiner's new main gig involved working fourteen hour days, but his obvious writing talents impressed the writers and producers, and they used some of Weiner's suggestions in the pilot.

After getting his first paying job as a writer, Weiner went on to write for popular comedies like *Becker*. When Weiner wasn't working on his main gig, he spent his free time in the mornings and at night working on a side project.

This time, he didn't expect it to pay the bills. He had an idea for a little television show about the lives of a group of successful but unhappy advertising executives during the 1950s and 60s.

In the book *Getting There*, he tells Gillian Zoe Segal about this side project:

 I always wanted to create my own show, so I started researching my "advertising project" in my spare time. It was like having a mistress. I worked on it at night or during my off-hours when I was not with my family."

Weiner faced a new problem. Putting in 14-hour days at the main gig didn't leave him enough free time or energy to get the words down on the page at night. Weiner could have put his big idea on the shelf, but like a lot of creative masters, he didn't quit.

Instead, Weiner used earnings from his main gig to hire a transcriber to record his ideas. He also hired a researcher to help him unearth small details that gave his side project more authenticity. Weiner says:

 I paid people to do research, inundated myself with material, and even hired a writer's assistant to dictate to because I was too tired to type (it also freed my imagination). When I finished the script, I felt like it was something special."

When Weiner wasn't working on his main thing, he lived with his side project. He carried a script for *Mad Men* everywhere he went. He showed it to his colleagues and David Chase, the director, creator and writer of *The Sopranos*.

Chase was so impressed by the script that he hired Weiner as a writer and supervising producer. He said about Weiner's idea,

 It was lively, and it had something new to say . . . Here was someone who had written a story about advertising in the 1960s, and was

looking at recent American history through that prism."

At first, while working on *The Sopranos*, Weiner put his script aside for the most part. Later when *The Sopranos* drew to an end, Weiner pitched his big idea to producers on the side.

Before the final season of *The Sopranos* aired, Weiner sold *Mad Men* to the ABC television network because, "They were trying to make a splash and wanted to do something new."

Finally realising his dream, Weiner became show runner for *Mad Men* and filmed 13 episodes of season one. What started out as a side project became a hit TV show that ran for seven seasons and won 16 Emmys as well as four Golden Globes.

The Unexpected Origin of this Book

I started writing this book as a side project. I've always wanted to learn about creativity and to find out how great writers, musicians, artists, filmmakers and creative masters find and deliver their big ideas.

I spent two years reading articles and books about the lives and working habits of creative people like Albert Einstein, Leonardo da Vinci and more modern creative masters like Steve Jobs, Twyla Tharp and Matthew Weiner.

I didn't set out to write a book about creativity, but the more I read about these people, the more I used what I learnt as fuel for my writing projects.

I also kept everything I discovered in a file on my computer and without knowing it I began to assemble the spine of a book piece by piece.

While gathering this information, I continued working on my main gig, which included finishing a collection of short stories, finishing a book about productivity and working full-time.

In the summer of 2015, I reviewed the information and research. I gathered it in one place and realised I'd accumulated enough for a book about creativity. The sheer volume of information suggested to me I had an idea to complete.

I faced a choice. I could have continued writing fiction in my free time or I could turn my unearthed ideas and research into a nonfiction book about creativity.

I decided to turn a little side project that had been bubbling away at the back of my mind into a big one. So I began to organise my ideas and research relevant themes, and I took time out from whatever else I was working on to write this book.

I share this humble origin so you can see side projects are an important pursuit for anyone who wants to become more creative.

Now let's explore how you can get more from your creative side projects:

Switch to Your Side Project When You Need a Break

I love creative side projects because they help me procrastinate and still get things done. They help me avoid feeling like I want to pull my hair out when I'm working at my main gig.

They also help me cultivate new creative habits without taking massive risks or investing a lot of time and money into a single idea.

The next time you're struggling with your main gig and think, "Oh God, I just don't have the energy, the passion or any good ideas to face into this today," pick up your side project and work on that instead.

Do it for five minutes, do it for an hour, or do it for an entire day. Then return to your main gig with the energy of someone who's just back from a refreshing holiday in the sun.

If you're lucky enough to love your main gig, switching gives you a much-needed break from a troublesome idea and enables you to practise your creative skills in a different way. You could even be nudging your career along like Weiner did.

Experiment Without Expectation

Consider your side project a creative experiment that will give you a new perspective on your craft. Defer critical decisions like a final deadline or the ending of a story.

You've got a chance to become tolerant of the ambiguity that comes with not having reached a decision or closed a loop; so seize it!

Practise accepting the discomfort of having an open loop, an unreached decision or a final cut: all luxuries you probably don't have while at your main gig. Use your side projects to practise facing your fears.

Avoid pressing hard for a great idea or for something you must use. You're free to abandon reason, logic and even clarity. Be reckless and bold with your ideas.

If you fail or if the experiment blows up in your face, this isn't a catastrophe because you haven't invested all of your emotional, financial or creative resources in your side project.

Break It Down

You shouldn't feel intimidated by the scale and ambition of your side project.

If you do, break your side project down into little treats you enjoy or that offer a relief when your main gig is turning sour.

Today, it's enough to read up on the background for your television script. Tomorrow, it's sufficient to transcribe your notes. It's enough because there are no expectations. It's only you and your ideas.

Here's a caveat:

You must progress your side project in some small way and not just hold it in the back of your mind or talk about it with friends over a beer.

Matthew Weiner would never have filmed *Mad Men* if all he did was tell his friends he had a great idea for a television show and that he'll get around to working on it someday.

Don't Quit Your Day Job (Yet)

Do you have bills, small kids or a spouse to provide for? If you quit your job because you want to spend all day alone with your side project, expect to hear from your bank manager.

Here's the thing:

Your main gig is giving you a fantastic opportunity to play with a side project early in the morning or late at night. Even if it doesn't fire you up, it's keeping the lights on at home.

You have freedom and licence to work on your side project without fear of failure because your main gig is taking care of business.

But what if you can afford to quit the day job and work on your side project all day?

Once you do this, your side project becomes your new job.

You'll have to finish it, ensure it pays the bills and keeps the lights on. You won't be free to take as many creative risks or experiment, and there will be things about your side project that you won't enjoy, but you'll have to do them if you want to feed your family.

While You're There, Work Hard at It

Would Matthew Weiner have become a successful television writer for *The Sopranos* (thus earning the respect and mentorship of David Chase) if he had obsessed about *Mad Men* on set and paid no attention to the television show he was being paid to create?

Probably not.

When you're at your main gig, devote yourself to it.

Then, consider how you can use the skills and resources you're acquiring during the nine-to-five to advance your side project in some small way.

Perhaps you're a marketer, and you can use what you learn on the job to sell more of your art?

Perhaps, like Weiner you're a television writer, and you can use your connections to pitch your ideas to other producers.

Maybe you're a web designer, and you're able to use your design skills to create a website for your side project.

Even if your main gig has nothing to do with your side project or your art, use what they pay you (after the bills are taken care of) to hire an editor, designer, producer or mentor and buy the materials you need for your side project.

Combining Your Experiences

Work on different things at the same time, and you'll connect them in exciting and unexpected ways.

You'll form these connections when you're dreaming, exercising, meditating, eating, listening to music, in the shower and so on. All you have to do is be open to capturing these connections when they occur to you.

When a connection bubbles to the surface of your mind or when a breakthrough in your side project occurs to you while you're working on your main gig, write it down in your notepad and carry on with your job.

Your subconscious will take care of the rest.

At the very least, use your day-to-day experiences on the job to lend credibility to your art.

American writer Charles Bukowski (1920-1994) spent much of his early life working at a menial job he hated for the United States postal service. He turned many of his experiences on the job into source materials (characters, anecdotes, descriptions) for his breakout 1971 novel *Post Office*.

His protagonist/alter-ego in that story even says while bored on the job, "Maybe I'll write a novel...And then I did."

Organise Your Ideas as You Go

The problem with side projects is you won't always have a lot of free time to work on them.

You must be able to access your research and ideas for your side project quickly and easily. A dedicated file on your computer is a great way to do this. That said, hand-written notes work too.

I keep a file on my computer for each side project, which contains my ideas, conversation snippets, photographs, outlines and more.

When I think of something and don't have access to this file, I write down the thought and put it with the rest of my ideas for my side project at the end of the day.

I also reread each of these ideas at the end of the week to see what I've got.

It takes only a few minutes, but it saves me hours of combing through old research later on.

I feel confident knowing my research is organised and that I can focus on the most important thing – whatever is in front of me.

Kick-start Your Side Project Today

Side projects are the friend of anyone who wants to become more creative and whatever stage you're at in your creative career, they'll help you invest in your future. What you practise for just an hour or two today, could change your life tomorrow – or in seven years.

It took Weiner seven years from the time he started work on his side project until *Mad Men* appeared on our television screens. Weiner's story shows how a side project kept on the back burner can become the main thing over time.

Remember that burnout can happen to you even if you enjoy your job or career. If you feel exhausted, irritable, or cynical about your work, re-invigorate yourself with a side project.

Think of your side project as a long-term investment.

Although it might not pay out today or tomorrow, you could reap rewards down the road as Weiner did with *Mad Men*.

If you're a musician in a group, experiment with your solo work in your free time. If you're a nonfiction writer, work on your fiction in the evenings.

If you're a filmmaker for a hit TV show (Congratulations!), work on whatever else inspires you early in the morning or late at night.

What you have on the side today, you'll dine out with tomorrow.

Creative Takeaways

- Start a side project today and give yourself permission to fail.
- Is your main gig turning your hair grey? Take out an old idea, dust it off and play with it a while.

8

GO TO WAR AGAINST YOUR FEARS

"There is only one thing that makes a dream impossible to achieve: the fear of failure."
– Paulo Coelho

It wasn't supposed to be like this.

When you aspired to become an artist, you imagined publishing work that gets better with age and your peers telling each other, "Now there's talent!"

Instead, when you try to create, you feel paralysed.

You don't know if your big idea will survive, and every moment you spend breathing life into it is a struggle.

What you eventually create takes longer than you planned, and it fills you with disappointment.

Here's what happened to me:

When I started writing in public for the first time, I worried how people close to me would react.

What would my friends say if I mined our confidence for a story?

What would my mother think if I wrote about sex?

Will people think I'm odd if I describe how I get up at dawn to write and that I sometimes prefer being alone in a small room with a big idea to the company of others?

I felt like an imposter.

I thought, "*Who are you to call yourself a writer? Get out of here before I call the police!*"

My fears held me back from being honest on the blank page because I was worried about what other people would think.

These selfish fears held me back from my best mistakes, from unexpected opportunities and from becoming a better writer.

I should have written about the party where I drank too much and embarrassed myself, the time I got fired and what happened next.

I should have shown my warts because that's the job. I should have known I was facing one of the common fears everyone with a big idea faces.

I'm Afraid of Starting

Starting is tough.

When I was in my early twenties, I told people I wanted to write a book. What I didn't tell them about was my problem.

For years, I couldn't start writing. I'd open up my word processor and then switch to my internet browser for research. I'd answer my email or see if there was something I wanted to buy on Amazon. Afterwards, I'd check my bank balance and feel depressed.

It went on like this until I disappeared down a rabbit

hole of meaningless web searches and doing anything but my most important work.

I wasn't writing anything. I believed I wasn't ready to write, and I needed some anointed mentor to pull me aside and say, "Bryan, now is your time."

Jealous of the success of others and sick of my lack of progress, I joined a fiction and nonfiction writing workshop in Dublin. On the second evening, the instructor said every student had to submit a short story.

I was afraid of starting, but I was even more afraid of being found out.

I hadn't written a short story in years, but I didn't want the class or the instructor to know.

A writer in a writing class who doesn't write, is a fraud.

I went home, and I wrote. I wrote that night and the night after that. I wrote until I finished my first short story. It was terrible – the instructor told me this later – but that didn't matter.

I had taken the first step towards facing my fear of starting.

How to Conquer This Fear

If you're having trouble starting, remember: It's your job to turn up and work on your big idea.

Be brutal with the activities filling your day. No, I'm not suggesting unemployment or divorce. Instead, eliminate the non-essential:

- Quit Facebook.
- Delete the email app from your phone.
- Watch television only on the weekend.
- Turn off notifications on your computer.

- Disable your internet access while you work on your ideas.

Protect your free time and concentrate on developing a habit of creating every day.

I learnt how to start by creating subtle mental triggers for writing. These include brewing coffee, setting a timer for how long I want to write and disconnecting from the internet.

My routine for becoming a writer involves doing this at the same time each evening or morning. It's a ritual, and that means I don't have to think about starting.

To the outsider, this routine looks dull, but it helps me write. Writing is more exciting than anything else I could do with my free time.

Once you've learned how to start, consider it a victory to work on your ideas for 10 minutes without getting distracted. The next day, aim for 15 minutes. The day after, work on your ideas for 20 minutes.

Let these small personal victories accumulate over time and you will conquer this fear. You'll know you're winning when it feels like your ideas are taking over your life. That's a better problem—trust me.

I'm Afraid I'm Not Good Enough

Before writing this series, I published two books: *A Handbook for the Productive Writer* (now called *The Savvy Writer's Guide to Productivity*) and a novella *Poor Brother, Rich Brother*.

I am nobody.

While writing the former, I was afraid others would ask, "What right do you have to explain how to be productive?"

I still think that.

I also knew I'd spent hours researching productivity methods and studying how artists work. I'd read dozens of books by authors explaining how they work, and I knew enough to organise my thoughts into a book.

Even though I am nobody, I gave myself permission to write a book because we've got to start somewhere.

Today, I'm afraid of hugely successful writers like Stephen King, Neil Gaiman and J.K. Rowling. They can write or create far more substantial works per year than I ever could in a lifetime.

King, for example, writes at least one novel per year, and his books are hardly thin. Books like *The Stand* and *The Shining* are more than 500,000 words long, while J.K. Rowling has created an entire world that people have made films about and even created a theme park to bring her fictional world to life.

I wonder, why bother? Shouldn't I just leave things in King's and Rowling's more than talented hands and stop wasting my time?

If you're not a writer, perhaps your negative self-talk goes a little a like this:

- Why can't I think of anything creative?
- I'll never be able to think of a unique idea.
- I'm too old/too young/not talented enough to learn how to play my favourite instrument.
- I'm afraid of performing in public because I'll forget what comes next.

Let's fix that.

How to Conquer This Fear

I'd like to tell you negative self-talk disappears when you're standing on the foundations of experience and success, but even creative masters doubt themselves. The Dutch post-impressionist painter Vincent Van Gogh (1853-1890) struggled with self-doubt throughout his entire life. His advice?

 If you hear a voice within you say you cannot paint, then by all means paint and that voice will be silenced."

Become aware of your negative self-talk and listen to it. If your mind is a blue sky, negative self-talk is nothing more than black clouds that you can watch as they pass.

Accept negative self-talk for what it is – just talk. If this is a struggle, ask yourself:

- Was there a trigger that precipitated this negative self-talk?
- Am I looking for affirmation from someone else?
- Can I acknowledge my imperfections for what they are: part of the shared human experience?

Indulge for a few minutes in this self-reflection. Then, set this negative self-talk aside by journaling, meditating or exercising.

Then you should be ready to sit down and do your work. Give yourself permission to create. When it feels difficult or overwhelming, remind yourself every artist must start somewhere and now is your time.

To imagine you are a creative poet, writer or musician is

to become that person. So, push forward one word, one idea or one beat at a time.

You're almost there.

I'm Afraid They'll Judge Me

"What will my mother say when she finds out I'm writing about sex?"

"What will my friends think when they catch me describing the world and its ugly imperfections?"

"What will my wife/husband do when they see themselves in my work?"

I don't like writing pieces like this. They're hard work, and they're more personal than a guide or a review. I almost deleted this chapter several times.

What's to enjoy about revealing a job didn't work out, I was lazy, and my work failed?

What must you think of me?

New artists find it difficult to separate their personal lives from their work, and they often regard criticism of their work as a reflection on their character.

Fiction writers, for example, often face a disconcerting moment when they reread a piece and find parts of their personal life scattered on the page.

I'll never forget the first time my wife read a short story I'd submitted into a competition. She asked if she was the woman in the story. I didn't admit it then, but she was right.

How to Conquer This Fear

The judgement of your peers and sometimes of people you trust is an essential part of the creative process if you want to overcome your weaknesses.

American film director Andrew Stanton (b. 1965) – he of *WALL–E* and *Finding Nemo* – tells his team at Pixar studios to "fail early and fail fast."

Stanton and his team rely on critical feedback to adjust problems in their work head-on and to avoid costly mistakes in their films down the road. He says,

> You wouldn't say to somebody who is first learning to play the guitar, 'You better think really hard about where you put your fingers in the guitar neck before you strum, because you only get to strum once and that's it. And if you get that wrong, we're going to move on."

Having your work judged is never easy, but the more you reveal your work to the world, the better you'll get at separating yourself from it.

Then when someone in the know criticises your work, know that it's about your work and not about a personal failing of yours.

I'm Afraid of Finishing

When I was in my mid-twenties, I spent years struggling to finish anything. I wrote dozens of short stories and abandoned them. I thought of articles I wanted to write for newspapers; I researched them and then I never finished them.

There wasn't any one moment when I learnt how to complete my work and become a writer. Instead, I got a job as a journalist writing for a newspaper. There, I had to finish my articles by a deadline because if I didn't my editor would have fired me.

I know this because he called me into his office after I missed a deadline and told me so.

Finishing is harder than starting for another reason too.

Many artists say they feel a certain sense of emptiness when their book, painting, album or big idea is finished. You live with something for hours, days, months or even years, fantasise about the moment it's over and then when that time comes, you feel bereft.

How to Conquer This Fear:

I stopped polishing my articles until they were perfect and I finished them.

On more than one occasion, my editor sent the pieces back to me, saying I'd left out an important paragraph or my introduction needed reworking. Other times, the sub-editors of the paper revised my articles entirely.

Having my work being taken apart felt brutal, but at least I was getting paid to write, and I learnt more from finishing my articles than from endlessly reworking them.

If the finish line feels far away, break your work down into smaller pieces that you can finish one by one. Instead of finishing an album, finish one song. Instead of writing a screenplay, write a scene. Repeat until you finish.

Know that you must break away from your creative project in the end and release it into the world. Then, erect a boundary between who you are as a person and the big idea you've finished.

Actor Johnny Depp (b. 1963) is just one of the many successful actors and actresses who erect such barriers.

 I would rather stay as ignorant as possible about the result of anything because once you're done playing that character, it's really not your business anymore."

Depp, like many writers and musicians who dislike listening to their old works or rereading their novels, doesn't watch himself in past films. Depp like many creative masters stands apart from his big ideas and because of this, he is free to grow in different directions.

I'm Afraid of Failure and Rejection

Most artists have stacks of unpublished essays, articles and stories in their drawer, notebook or on their computer.

Your personal slush pile could be a stack of paintings, recordings or something else entirely. Know that it's all part of the creative process.

Every creative work isn't meant to succeed. Not everything Shakespeare (1564-1616) wrote was a hit. His plays *Troilus and Cressida* and *Timon of Athens*, which he wrote at the height of his creative powers, are far less popular and acclaimed than *Hamlet* and *King Lear*.

Some pieces serve as markers for your journey towards becoming a better artist or as evidence that you're doing the work.

How to Conquer This Fear:

I was rejected more times than I care to admit over the past week. I contacted five authors I admire with interview requests. Four of them said no.

I asked several podcasting experts for their advice for a guest blog post I'm writing. Half of them didn't reply.

I pitched guest posts at three big blogs, two of which said no.

People are going to reject your ideas, and that's OK. Rejection waits for you at the beginning, in the middle and at the end of your big ideas. It goes where you go. Everybody who succeeds gets rejected.

By turning up and creating, you cut through your fear of rejection. Even if some people reject your work, others will embrace it. The next editor or patron you pitch might accept your ideas. You could win the next contest. Your next interview request might be granted.

To become an artist, you must create today. You must create now. You create like your life depends on it.

Because it does.

I'm Afraid of Success

When the World Chess Championship began in 1990, Garry Kasparov (b. 1953) was a success. His opponent at the championship was Kasparov's long-time rival Anatoly Karpov, and the odds were in Kasparov's favour.

The two chess players competed in 24 games over three months, with 12 taking place in New York and 12 in Lyon, France.

Although Kasparov began the competition strongly, he began to commit mistakes. He lost the seventh game and, at the close of the first half of the tournament, the men were tied.

After losing a big game, Kasparov looked fragile and afraid. He was in real danger of losing his world title.

The *New York Times* reported, "Mr Kasparov had lost confidence and grown nervous in New York."

Instead of quitting, Kasparov turned to a secret mental

strategy for conquering his fear. When he sat down at the board for a decisive match in France, Kasparov puffed up his chest, and adopted a fiercely aggressive playing style. He acted as if he were confidence itself.

Chess player Josh Waitzkin wrote:

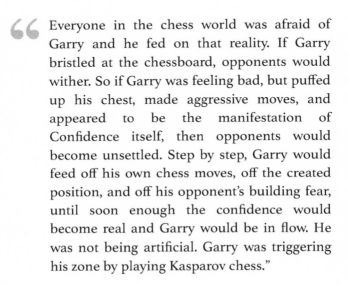 Everyone in the chess world was afraid of Garry and he fed on that reality. If Garry bristled at the chessboard, opponents would wither. So if Garry was feeling bad, but puffed up his chest, made aggressive moves, and appeared to be the manifestation of Confidence itself, then opponents would become unsettled. Step by step, Garry would feed off his own chess moves, off the created position, and off his opponent's building fear, until soon enough the confidence would become real and Garry would be in flow. He was not being artificial. Garry was triggering his zone by playing Kasparov chess."

Through acting like a champion, Kasparov subsequently won the sixteenth, eighteenth and twentieth games and retained his title as World Chess Champion.

How to Conquer This Fear

To overcome your fear of success, adopt the Kasparov mind-set. Force yourself to behave like you're full of great ideas; you know what you're doing, and you've already won.

If you're working on a novel and you're afraid of what will happen when you achieve a breakthrough, ask yourself, "How would a great novelist and storyteller write this?"

If you're composing a track for an album and the hook scares you, ask yourself, "How would a world-class musician play this?"

Be bold with your answers. Push past that place of discomfort and fear until you reach a place where your success is inevitable.

Offer no quarter for self-doubt. When you enter into the mental zone that belongs to the victorious, you won't fear success; you'll relish it.

Seizing Victory

Each morning when I sit down in front of the blank page, I feel the heavy paws of fear on my shoulders pressing me down, his cold breath in my ear, his raspy voice telling me, "You're not good enough."

I step forward one word, one sentence, one paragraph, one idea at a time. I force myself to press "Publish" because this is a war I must win. Then, I reach out to others and show them what I've done.

When they don't believe me, I show them my wounds.

Do you know what happened when I did this for the first time?

Nothing.

Our would-be audience is more concerned with the problems in their lives than anything you and I are too afraid to say or to finish.

The problem isn't what people will think of our work or that we're damaged or too ambitious. It's convincing our would-be audience that our big ideas are worth their time.

Go to war against your fears.

If victory were easy, the conquest wouldn't be worth it, but your struggle and frustrations are simply opportunities in disguise. You will unmask them for what they are during your bold march forward.

What you must never do is retreat because filling a blank page or a virgin canvas is too much work.

What you must never do is to let difficult moments overwhelm you and prevent you from seeking out new ways to improve your craft.

What you must never do is quit on a big idea because it's more elusive than you thought.

So create, damn it.

Don't hold back.

And put your ideas out there.

Because each idea you fire is an arrow into the belly of the beast.

Creative Takeaways

- Work on your idea for just 10 minutes today, 15 minutes tomorrow and 20 the day after that. Through the power of small daily wins, you can accomplish more on the blank page or virgin canvas.
- If you haven't accomplished anything in a while, finish just one of your creative projects, however small. Through finishing, you'll discover more about what to create next.

9

LASTING CHANGE, JUST AROUND THE CORNER

"Art is the triumph over chaos."
– John Cheever

It's been five years since I turned 30 and picked myself up off the bathroom floor. My beard is more grey, and my hairline has receded further up my head, but I've faced some of my fears.

I long ago left the job I hated. I found another job, lost that one and then moved into a career that rewards me. Outside of work, I push myself to write 1,000 words a day, to publish honest articles and stories on a blog once a week and in books like this one.

These are my choices. Some of them were good, and some were bad, but it's better to move forwards than to be trapped in a rut.

I won't lie, all this honesty and the constant hunt for ideas is a challenge that sometimes leaves me cowering.

I still fall down, face painful mistakes and feel like giving up. Last year instead of publishing a book that was almost ready, I wasted three months rewriting an old book because I was afraid of what I'd written.

When this happens, I lean on my habits.

I don't try to knock out *War and Peace* in a weekend; sometimes writing 500 words is enough. I push forwards until I gain momentum on difficult creative projects.

I practise strengthening my mind and body through meditation and long-distance running because depression, anxiety and ill-health are an anathema to thinking big.

Even if I don't think of a good idea today or tomorrow, I know with the right preparation and a consistent daily practise, I'll find an idea I can use in the end.

I count on these daily habits as ordinary blessings that lead to greater things.

I haven't discovered some ancient secret or transformed myself into a zebra who can magically change its stripes. Instead, I realised that creative masters from the arts, business, technology and more will help us become more creative...if we look hard enough.

Look at how McCartney mined his dreams for songs, how Dali held himself to a routine so he was free to paint or even how Weiner relied on an assistant to help him write while balancing a main job.

We just have to be brave enough to walk the path mapped by these creative masters.

Look, most people believe creativity is a natural ability you either have or lack, but now you and I know to be creative is to embark on a journey that nourishes and strengthens us with every step.

What Your Journey Looks Like

Start by finding out what you feel passionate about.

People say it's a "passion project" when they're describing a film they had to create, a book they were compelled to write or an album they needed to record even though they'd no idea if their work would sell.

If you can find what you feel passionate about, you'll have a reason to get up, get out there and create.

Now don't get me wrong: When you're new at your craft, some people will wonder what you're doing and how you're spending your time.

It doesn't help that many of your early ideas serve as inward markers of your progress – that you turned up, that you tried – rather than something you can show.

Passion will keep you going when nothing else will. It's your lifeline during dark times. So pay attention to what drives and inspires you, to what you work on in the wee small hours. It's your guiding purpose.

Understand becoming more creative is as much about preparation and smart habits as it is about moments of divine inspiration.

Weiner spent years researching *Mad Men* on the side. Hill lay in bed each night mentally preparing with his imaginary council for the following day. Even Cheever used journal writing as a form of practice.

You'll have more time to prepare and create smart habits if you cull pointless activities from your life. Instead of watching another boxset on Netflix, learn how to ease yourself into your work and nudge yourself forwards, one idea, one side project at a time.

When you're starting off, you might need to support yourself with a "real job" and practise your passion projects around the margins of the day, in the morning before work or late at night.

That's OK.

Your job is a safety net that gives you freedom to learn what your audience wants and your craft demands each day. It gives you the freedom to jump without feeling over-whelmed by fear. Besides, lots of artists worked in other jobs when they were starting off.

T.S. Elliot worked in a bank. Ernest Hemingway was a journalist. Even Leonardo da Vinci took jobs as an advisor to his patrons and king.

If it helps, know that side projects (whether you consider them your job or what you do late at night or first thing in the morning) can lead to great and unexpected things.

I know it's tough.

Some days you will strike the page or canvas repeatedly, but nothing will spark. Your creative work is a grind, you put in hours alone in a room and produce nothing more than a useless sentence, a single chord or a sketch.

Your practise feels like a lonely cry in the dark.

And the reply?

A little voice whispering, "*What do you think you're doing?*"

King heard that same voice when he wrote an early draft of *Carrie*, but his wife helped him finish his first book. He was brave enough to listen to his mentor.

If you've struggled up till now, you too can change your stripes.

Turn up every day and practise your craft, even when you don't feel like it. Acknowledge your fears and self-doubt for what they are: Imposters in the way of your creative ideas.

Push past them!

If you need help practising or you want to save time, pick a creative master to follow. Using their guidance, you can avoid many of the potholes and wrong turns that lie before you.

Remember to be bold with your creative experiments, challenge your assumptions, put one foot in front the other and keep going.

The road ahead is long and winding, but you are bolder, stronger and more powerful than you can imagine.

THE POWER OF CREATIVITY (BOOK 2)

AN UNCOMMON GUIDE TO MASTERING YOUR INNER GENIUS AND FINDING NEW IDEAS THAT MATTER

BRYAN COLLINS

THE POWER OF
CREATIVITY

AN UNCOMMON GUIDE TO
MASTERING YOUR INNER GENIUS
AND FINDING NEW IDEAS THAT MATTER
(BOOK 2)

1

THE RIVER

"Creativity is like carrying a bucket to the river."
– Unknown

The above quote is an old saying about creativity from the Far East.

The unprepared man or woman who goes down to the riverbank without a bucket finds it harder to draw from the well-spring of ideas because he or she can cup up only so much water in their hands before it flows through their fingers.

Prepared people who bring buckets to the river quench their thirst, fill their buckets and take generous helpings back to their friends, families or peers.

In the West, people concerned about creativity care less about buckets and more about those moments of inspiration when an idea arrives as if from above.

No wonder the creative process and figuring out where great ideas come from feels so mystifying.

I've felt fascinated and mystified by the creative process for years. I wanted to discover more about how past creative masters like Leonardo da Vinci, Henri Matisse and Albert Einstein and modern creative masters like Steve Jobs, Elizabeth Gilbert and John Cleese found their big ideas.

I set out to discover their insights into the creative process and whether they knew a secret hidden from the rest of us.

I found that creative masters fill their buckets with hundreds of little ideas–the ones that seem crazy, outlandish or foolish–and then they distil what they find into a single, powerful, big idea.

You too can find little ideas (and later distil them into big ones that matter) if you come down to the river prepared. In the pages to come, I will show you how.

Who This Book is For

This book is the *second in a three-part series* about creativity that I wrote for new writers, musicians, filmmakers, and artists.

The first book in this series–*The Power of Creativity: Learning How to Build Lasting Habits, Face Your Fears and Change Your Life*–was for writers, artists and musicians who felt adrift.

This second book is for anyone who has asked questions such as: "How can I make something genuinely original?" or "How can I get more ideas?" or "What's the best way to focus on my ideas and just let them flow?"

You don't need to be a genius or possess some mystical talent to become more creative at your chosen craft. Instead, you just need to know where to look for ideas. If you're a writer, musician or artist wondering where to look, this book will help you.

Over the chapters ahead, you'll gain chosen techniques for generating ideas. You'll also discover how to adopt the mindsets of creative masters such as Einstein, Matisse and Jobs to get better at your craft.

In each chapter, I'll draw on scientific and academic studies alongside the experiences of past creative masters so you can unlock fresh thinking.

This book is as much practical as it is informative. At the end of each chapter, I'll also provide "Creative Takeaways" you can use to improve the quality and quantity of your little (and big) ideas.

Fresh Thinking and Great Ideas

So where can you find great ideas?

Well, they're everywhere . . . if you know where to look.

And look we shall.

In this book, I'll cover how to capture free-flowing thoughts, organise your thinking and come up with lots of little ideas faster using proven creative techniques from academia and the toolboxes of accomplished writers and artists.

The good news is you don't need to be an expert in your chosen field or craft to look for or even to come up with little or big ideas; in fact being an outsider gives you a unique perspective.

There's more . . .

When you're an outsider, you're more open to experimenting with form and substance, and that open-mindedness will help you inject a little bit of Matisse or Einstein's thinking into your work.

Then, things are going to get ambiguous.

You see here's the open secret about creativity:

There are no original ideas. Old ideas are simply retold and combined in different ways.

Now I don't want you to be accused of being a thief, so I'll show you how to use other people's ideas without compromising your sense of ethics (or getting sued), as well as how to build on the work of your creative heroes.

And then, are you open to asking and answering a few difficult questions?

I ask because cultivating an intense sense of curiosity is an essential part of the creative process, and you can do it using a simple technique from the business world.

Successful creative people adopt a particular mindset. Call it flow, a fugue, or total immersion. I'll show you how creative masters turn on and off this mindset at will and how you can do the same.

In the end, unlocking fresh thinking means being open to the world around you. Later when the moment comes, you'll act on your ideas because you know there's lots to be done.

Now the river lies just ahead. Are you ready to dive in?

2

GO PROSPECTING FOR IDEAS

"To have a great idea, have a lot of them."
– Thomas Edison

I look for ideas at home and in work. I capture them on the bus, on the train and when I wake at 3:00 a.m.

I don't write down ideas while driving the car because that's bad karma.

I write in the morning, at night and sometimes in the afternoons.

I capture ideas with my phone, on notepads and Moleskines (I once even wrote about Moleskines.) and on the back of Post-Its.

I write ideas on scraps of paper (God I love a great piece of blank paper!), on the back of receipts, bills, bank statements and even on beer mats.

I record ideas while watching films and TV shows and cooking dinner. I write online, and I write in the woods. I write ideas down while connected and disconnected, plugged in, unplugged, wired and stone-cold sober.

Hey, Hemingway! It's always easier stone-cold sober.

I capture ideas on laptops and computers old and new. I write on Macs and PCs; I write with broken pens and unsharpened pencils.

I write ideas into the notes app on my phone, in Word-Press, on Medium, Twitter, Facebook, LinkedIn and in every other box that fills my screen.

I write with broken things about broken things and for broken people. I write for myself.

I write down ideas until my head aches and my heart spins.

So, I take a break . . .

Where was I?

I'm on the toilet with one leg hunched over the other, a pen in my hand and a big idea to chase down.

"Come catch me, Bryan..."

I'm trying, baby, slow down!

I write for food. I write for money. I write to pass the time. I write when I'm bored, lonely, angry or tired. Some days, I can't think of anything at all.

And that's always worse.

I consider new ideas in my head, and people turn and ask me, "What are you thinking about?"

"Don't disturb me, I've got an idea man, can't you see?"

"You're so crazy," they say.

But I don't care. I just write on and on.

It never stops.

Where and When to Write Down Ideas

I'm telling you all of this because I want you to become fastidious about recording whatever pops into your mind, whether it's in a notebook, an app or on a piece of blank paper.

Many artists keep a notebook beside their beds in case they dream of an idea during their sleep, wake up and want to capture it on paper before they forget.

You don't need a pretty or expensive notebook, and don't worry about recording the wrong things. Instead, write down five to ten ideas each morning.

If you're uncomfortable writing, use a dictaphone or the recorder on your phone to capture melodies and fragments that pop into your mind.

Your goal is simply to practise coming up with ideas more frequently. Doing this trains your monkey mind to focus on the possibilities around you.

If you write ideas down every day, you'll increase the chances of having at least one or two actionable creative ideas by the end of the week, whereas the procrastinating artists who don't bother will reach the end of the week and find their buckets are empty.

But what if nothing useful or imaginative ever pops into your head? What if your imagination is barren and you can't fill your notebook or your recorder with ideas no matter how hard you try?

With some tenacity, you can drill down into your subconsciousness. Then, you can use three different powerful approaches for sifting through what you find and extracting a big or golden idea.

Approach 1: The Six Thinking Hats

In 1985, academic Edward de Bono (b. 1933) proposed the concept of *Six Thinking Hats* as a scientific way of coming up with more ideas that matter, faster. His Six Thinking Hats premise is easy to apply. Just consider your big idea while wearing six different metaphorical hats: a *Blue Hat, White Hat, Red Hat, Black Hat, Yellow Hat and a Green Hat.*

When you're tackling a new creative project, put on your *Blue Hat* to gain an overview of your big idea. Describe the process surrounding your idea. Consider what you want to explore, the problems you're having and your goal for the big idea in question.

Wearing my *Blue Hat* to describe this book, I can say it provides proven strategies for writers, musicians, artists and anyone who wants to overcome common creative challenges.

Next, don your imaginary *White Hat* and explain the facts about your big idea. Ask yourself what you know about your big idea and what facts do you possess?

I wore my *White Hat* when I wanted to write an initial outline of this book and evaluate what I knew about creativity and what I needed to learn or read up on.

Your metaphorical *Red Hat* is for articulating emotions. Ask yourself what your instinct or gut tells you about your big idea?

While tackling this project, my *Red Hat* thinking told me many people don't feel like they are creative. My gut told me they don't believe it's possible to become more creative.

Wear your *Black Hat* and view your big idea logically. Ask how you can approach your big idea in a sensible way? Your *Black Hat* thinking will help you become more critical of your big idea before you start working on it.

I wore my *Black Hat* and figured out that distilling my knowledge of creativity into applicable laws or strategies would make this book easier for people to read. I also found this approach would help me simplify the process of writing this book.

Wear your *Yellow Hat* to explore the benefits of your big idea. Ask what benefits your big idea offers and how will tackling it help you or your audience? Be optimistic and hopeful about how things will turn out.

In my case, I wore my *Yellow Hat* and figured out I could discover more about creativity if I wrote a book about it. My *Yellow Hat* thinking also told me I could help readers overcome common creative challenges.

Finally, wear your *Green Hat* for being more creative about your big idea. That means asking questions like: "How can I approach my big idea using fresh thinking?" and "What new ideas do I have?"

In my case, I read various books about creativity, and I came up with strategies that struck me as original but also as a summation of what I'd learnt during the research process.

Now that you know how to use DeBono's Six Thinking Hats, it's time to put this strategy into practise using freewriting.

The 50 Laws of Creativity (an early idea for this book)

Approach 2: Freewriting

Freewriting is the rapid, non-judgmental capturing of ideas on paper (or in your word processor) as they rise to the top of your mind. It's a technique artists can use to generate ideas that matter and overcome feeling blocked or uninspired.

Mark Levy, author of *Accidental Genius: Using Writing to Generate Your Best Ideas, Insight, and Content* defines freewriting as,

 A fast method of thinking onto paper that enables you to reach a level of thinking that's often difficult to attain during the course of a normal business day."

I've used freewriting in one form or another for years. The purpose is to get whatever is simmering in the back of your mind out of your head and onto a piece of paper. It doesn't matter if you what you write is daft or silly. The

point is only to capture whatever your subconsciousness has been wrestling.

Think of freewriting as exploratory drilling for oil–only it's better for the environment. It doesn't matter if you're not an accomplished writer because nobody is supposed to see the fruits of your freewriting sessions.

Instead, they serve as a way of thinking out loud on the page. When you finish freewriting, you can go back and reread what you wrote to see if there's anything you can extract. It's easy to sift through your subconscious for golden ideas through freewriting.

Write Fast

Don't give your brain a moment to pause or evaluate your thoughts. It doesn't matter if you make typos or spelling mistakes while freewriting–just keep getting the words out of your head and onto the blank page before the critical part of your brain has time to catch up.

Work Against a Limit:

I love limits because they give an artist confines within which to work. You can use a word count (the higher, the better), a deadline, or a timer.

I set a timer on my computer for 25 minutes, disconnect from the Internet, and freewrite as fast as I can without interruption. When the timer sounds, I take a break and evaluate my ideas.

Write What You See or Hear

Freewriting isn't the time for editing, so jot down random ideas, swear words, and off-topic points. If you get interrupted while freewriting, just write down that you were interrupted.

If you hear a dog barking on the street, and you remember that you need to feed your dog, write that down too. And if you think of an idea that has nothing to do with your creative challenge, follow your train of thought. These tangents are often the key to innovative work.

Express the Same Idea Multiple Ways

Expressing your idea multiple times helps you clarify it–and it's more productive than sitting around waiting for inspiration. Go back to your last idea and write it in a different way or from a different angle. If you're unsure how to do this, write down one of De Bono's questions and freewrite your answer.

Write the Way You Think

When you freewrite, keep it conversational and use everyday language. You're not here to impress anyone, and nobody is going to read what you're writing.

So, jump around from one topic to the next, swear and rage against your idea. Get the raw yolk of your big idea onto the page.

If the prospect of sitting down in front of the blank page induces nausea and you still need a way of drilling down for more ideas, fear not. There's another powerful creative strategy you can use.

Approach 3: Mind Mapping

Mind mapping is a proven and practical creative technique for organising your ideas, research and finding more ideas that matter.

Drawing a mind map, or mind mapping, is one of the best ways to establish links between your ideas and then see these connections in one place before you write.

Mind maps will also help you connect unrelated ideas, outline your work and save time creating. What's more, mind maps serve as useful memory aids, and they're ideal for visual thinkers.

As da Vinci said, "Everything is connected to everything else."

Modern science supports mind mapping as well.

Researchers at the University of Nottingham in the United Kingdom found drawings or visual representations (like mind maps) help people organise, break down and remember complex topics.

When to Use Mind Maps

Mind maps are ideal for almost any creative work. The only caveat of this technique is that each mind map should focus on a specific idea.

You can use mind mapping to see the overall structure of a book or a film, think through an idea before setting to work on it, review what you learnt and even to organise areas of your creative life.

Creating Your Mind Map

Think of your mind map as a tree. The central idea is the root, and the related ideas serve as branches.

To create your first mind map, start simple.

Get an A4 (or US letter size) white piece of paper and red, blue, green and black pens. Turn the paper on its side and write your idea or topic in the centre of the page.

From there, draw the connecting ideas.

Using your coloured pens, write connecting ideas along the branches, shooting out from the central idea. These branches or lines should be thicker at the root and grow thinner as they move out from the central idea.

Map out all that comes to mind and work on your mind map for 10 or 15 minutes without interruption.

Use Colours and Images

Red, blue, black, green markers will help you create a more visual and memorable mind map. You should see the central idea, the overall structure and how everything is connected at a glance.

You don't have to be great at drawing, either. It's enough to sketch simple images representing key ideas.

Don't fear making mistakes or obsess about the structure of your mind map. Instead, simply reorder your branches or draw another mind map if you need.

If you're using a whiteboard or digital tool, you can rearrange your mind map as you go.

Simplify Your Mind Maps

Although some mind mapping experts use complex mind maps, I find these are time consuming to create and use, particularly if you're unsure about how to use them for your creative work.

Experimenting with your mind maps is a good practise. You could try different pictures and colours. Or you could play with the shape, branch and order of your ideas.

Prune Your Mind Map

Your mind map will grow rapidly and in many directions. Like the artful gardener, it's your job to prune the tree and shape your mind map. When you've finished your first mind map, reorganise or remove what you don't need so you can understand it later on.

Mind Mapping Your Way to an Idea That Works

Even if your mind map looks pretty, it's useless if you avoid doing anything with it.

Have a plan for turning your mind map into something you can write or create. Or if your mind map serves as a visual aid keep it with you for a while. I also save digital mind maps in Evernote.

Remember, your mind map is a creative strategy, but it's not the work.

How I Used a Mind Map to Write This Chapter

Before writing my first draft of this part of the chapter, I created a mind map. My central idea was to answer the question, "What is mind mapping?"

After coming up with a central idea, I wrote down the main points of the chapter, based on what I'd read and researched.

Next, I expanded these main points and branched them out into sub-topics. I paid little attention to the order or structure of my ideas until I had finished.

After completing the first version of this mind map, I added colours and images to it. Next, I reorganised my mind map in a clockwise fashion. I put the introduction to the article at one o'clock, the "Why Mind Maps?" section at three o'clock, and so on.

Then I pruned or removed what I didn't need. Creating the map took about twenty minutes. Finally, I dictated this chapter by looking at my sheet and speaking into a microphone about the topics I'd mapped.

You don't have to create a mind map like this.

Some mind mapping aficionados put their central idea to the far left of the screen or page. Then, they branch out their ideas in a horizontal or a linear fashion, much like a Fishbone or cause and effect diagram.

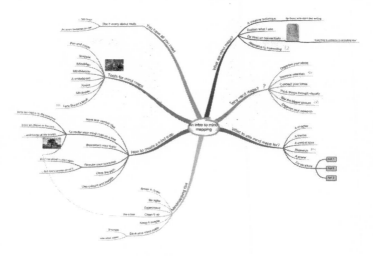

An early mind map for this book

What to Use for Creating Your Mind Maps

A number of digital tools and apps can help you create a great looking mind map (See the end of this book.), but analogue tools work too.

Limits encourage you to become more resourceful, so in this case, focus on your single idea. Pen, paper and multi-coloured pens are perfect mind mapping tools because they are affordable, available, and it's difficult to tinker with them.

I also like using a whiteboard for mind mapping because I can use an eraser to redraw and reconstruct parts of the mind map as I go. Again, I find it impossible to tinker with the settings of a whiteboard.

If you use pen and paper or a whiteboard for mind mapping, take a picture of your mind map with your phone and save it to your computer.

I save these pictures in Evernote alongside the rest of my research for books, blog posts or articles. I like advanced digital features as much as the next person, but the mind mapping tool you use is always less important than the process.

If you're mind mapping for the first time, I suggest going low-tech. Multi-coloured pens and a large sheet of paper are ideal.

All It Takes

Filling your bucket with great ideas is hard work, but you can extract more big or golden ideas from your subconscious and the world around you with the right strategy.

DeBono's Six Thinking Hats will help you ask better questions about whatever you're working on; freewriting will help you explore ideas deep in your subconscious and mind mapping will help organise your ideas before you get started.

Once you prospect for ideas and draw connections between what you find, you'll solve the problem of a barren imagination. You'll have tapped into your inner genius.

All it takes is practise.

Creative Takeaways

- Get a timer, a pen and some paper. Set the timer for thirty minutes and freewrite or mind map about a creative problem you're facing. Don't stop to edit yourself or read your work until the buzzer sounds.

- During your freewriting or mind mapping session, wear each one of De Bono's Six Thinking Hats to increase the quantity and improve the quality of your ideas.

3

EXPERIMENT WITH FORM AND SUBSTANCE

"A song is like a saddle: you ride it for a while, and if it's the right kind of song you can sing it for the rest of your life."
– Glen Hansard

In 1887, Henri Matisse (1869-1954) began to study law and worked as a court administrator in Le Cateau-Cambrésis in Paris, but the trajectory of his life changed after a bout of appendicitis two years later. While recovering, he had little to do. So his mother bought Matisse a box of paints.

"From the moment I held the box of colours in my hands, I knew this was my life. I threw myself into it like a beast that plunges towards the thing it loves," he said.

Matisse abandoned law to study art and work under artists such as the painter John Peter Russell. He created still life and landscape paintings before moving to more impressionistic works.

He first made his name as an expressionist painter in the vein of Paul Cézanne and Marcel Duchamp. Critics regarded Matisse as an extremist and a wild beast or a fauve.

Later, he became famous for paintings like *Music* and *The Dance* and for his sculptures. Throughout his career, his works were compared endlessly with those by his younger rival Pablo Picasso.

American art collector and critic Leo Stein said about Matisse, "All his pictures were to give him a lot of trouble . . . He worked endlessly on his pictures until they were finished."

Matisse's troubles started each morning when he rose early to paint. He worked through the morning and again after lunch. In the evening, he enjoyed violin practise, a simple supper and an early bedtime. Throughout his career, he worked mostly alone, albeit with the help of assistants or models.

Matisse expressed himself using a paintbrush. Then he spent hours reworking his masterworks much like a writer editing a draft of their book.

In 1908, he said he wanted to create art "for every mental worker, for the businessman as well as the man of letters, for example, a soothing, calming influence on the mind, something like a good armchair which provides relaxation from physical fatigue."

As Matisse grew older and more successful, his critics regarded him as a creative master known for expressive colours and sensual works. He also explored other forms like drawings and sculptures and was able to bring insight from one form to the next.

"I sculpted as a painter," said Matisse, "I did not sculpt like a sculptor."

Then in 1941, Matisse was diagnosed with abdominal cancer.

The seventy-four-year-old artist underwent a serious operation in Lyon, France, which he didn't expect to survive. The surgery left Matisse chair and bed-bound, and he was unable to move about easily to paint or sculpt.

After this surgery, Matisse faced regular and complicated procedures to maintain his digestive system, and he recognised he was approaching the end of his life.

Many other creative people would have put their tools down and considered their most important work complete. Instead, Matisse regarded his declining health as a creative challenge to overcome and believed he was living a "second life."

In an echo of what had happened when his mother bought a twenty-year-old court administrator a box of paints, the elderly Matisse embraced a bolder artistic form, that of the scissors and coloured paper.

With the help of his assistant, he created a series of large colourful collages from cut paper and covered the walls of his bedroom with them. These cut-outs varied in colour and size, and some became room-sized works and murals.

Matisse published the first of these cut-outs as a series of illustrations in the book *Jazz* in 1947, and by 1948 he stopped painting altogether to focus on this form.

"I have attained a form filtered to its essentials," Matisse said about this new medium, which he used to express his joy of life.

His cut-outs portrayed lively compositions of dancers, musicians, swimmers, the circus, clowns, funerals and animals while others evoked images of death and war. They also represent a stunning and original chapter in the artist's long creative career and were relished by the critics of the day.

In 1951, an American critic said about Matisse's final works, "Never before has Matisse seemed to me so young."

Three years later Matisse died of a heart attack.

His life and art demonstrate how changing the form and substance of your creative works can enable better, bolder ideas and more inspired thinking.

Instead of holding too tightly to a way of working that you trust, consider how else you can express yourself and what you could do if your tools, resources, and even your health, were stripped away.

Why You Should Experiment With Form and Substance

Because Matisse told you so!

First, if you feel blocked or stuck, experimenting with form is a relieving remedy.

The constrictions of your chosen medium might not be ideal for expressing your idea, and a little experiment (like a cardboard cut-out) could help you find a better means of expression.

Ideas are everywhere; they are free flowing and formless. It's your job to form them into something tangible that engages your audience.

The form surrounding your big ideas will shift over the lifetime of your project, so don't solidify it prematurely because you want the work to be done.

Remember it's your responsibility to get your ideas in front of as many people as possible. Presenting your ideas in different forms will help your audience engage in a way that suits them.

This isn't derivative. It isn't lazy. And it's not uninspired.

What if, for example, a would-be reader of your book is

blind or prefers to listen to audio? Will you create an audio book so they can engage with your ideas?

It's also less exhausting to transform one good idea that works into a different form than it is to come up with a second idea. And a third. And a fourth.

You're doing yourself (and your audience) a great disservice by not considering how you might transform your idea into different forms to engage different people.

Finally, have you ever had the experience of studying under one teacher for months, only to find it all but impossible to learn what they were trying to teach?

Then later, another teacher addresses the same topic, and everything falls into place? In many cases, it's not that the second teacher was more accomplished than the first. Instead, listening to an idea multiple times, told in different ways, helps it sink in.

You can help your ideas sink in through creative experimentation.

How to Experiment with Form and Substance

Matisse experimented with canvas, clay and paper to express his ideas. Whether you're a writer, artist or musician, you have even more opportunities than Matisse to experiment with form and substance.

Austin Kleon (b. 1983) is an American writer, artist and poet who uses digital and analogue tools to experiment with form and substance.

Kleon composes poetry and creates art, but in an unusual way. He cuts out newspaper clippings and blackens the text with a felt-tip marker, leaving behind only certain words and phrases that form a poem.

He documents the process for creating his poems alongside the final result in his books, website and on Instagram. In his book *Steal Like an Artist*, Kleon wrote about his creative experiments,

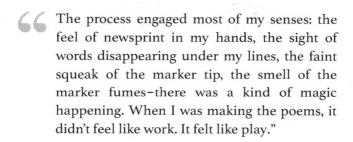 The process engaged most of my senses: the feel of newsprint in my hands, the sight of words disappearing under my lines, the faint squeak of the marker tip, the smell of the marker fumes—there was a kind of magic happening. When I was making the poems, it didn't feel like work. It felt like play."

Creative experimentation for writers was difficult in Matisse's time due to the costs of printing, but today digital tools enable any writer to experiment with the length and form of their works.

Hugh Howey (b. 1975) is an American science-fiction writer. In 2011, he began self-publishing a series of short stories about a dystopian, post-nuclear holocaust world.

His self-published short stories were a hit on Amazon, so Howey combined them into a novella and later a book called *Wool* before publishing the series *Silo*. He then released audiobooks of his popular series.

Howey understands that audiobooks enable new readers to find his book and that audio lends a sense of life and urgency to his work.

In 2012, he signed a traditional book publishing deal and 20th Century Fox/Lionsgate bought the film rights to his book.

Howey cares less about the old rules of publishing books; his mission is to get his stories out in front of as many people as possible. On his blog, he wrote,

You are writing for the reader, who is your
ultimate gatekeeper. Get your work in front of
them, even if it's one at a time, one reader a
month or year."

But what if you compose music?

Take heart from how Glen Hansard (b. 1970), Markéta
Irglová (b. 1988) and John Carney (b. 1972) transformed their
music and stories.

From Ireland, Hansard is the frontman of The Frames
and one-half of folk rock duo, The Swell Season with
Markéta Irglová, while John Carney is an Irish film and TV
writer.

In 2007, Carney wrote a movie script about a struggling
thirty-something busker who falls in love with a folk singer
and single mother from the Czech Republic. He invited his
friend Hansard (they played together in *The Frames* years
ago) and Irglová to star in the film, for which they also wrote
the soundtrack.

The events on-screen mirrored events off-screen in that
Hansard and Irglová were, for a time, a real-life couple and
they appeared to portray characters similar to themselves.

The film became a commercial success, and Hansard
and Irglová won an Oscar for "Falling Slowly" from the
soundtrack.

Although *Once* is a worldwide hit today, it's worth
remembering this film started as a small indie project shot
over three weeks with a modest budget of just over
EUR112,000.

What's even more significant is that Hansard and Irglová
first released the music comprising *Once* as their self-titled
Swell Season record and sold only 300 copies.

After they had the attention of an audience, they rereleased the album with a different cover and marketed it as a soundtrack for *Once*, and it went gold.

Hansard told music magazine *Pitchfork*,

 But I couldn't believe that this record I put out with Mar, that I was really proud of, only sold 300. Then six months or a year later it gets rereleased as the *Once* record. Four days ago I just heard that it went gold over here. That's half a million fucking records! That's insane! That is fucking insane. And all we did was change the cover [laughs]."

The team behind *Once*, like many creative masters, know the value of repurposing great ideas.

Irish playwright Enda Walsh transformed *Once* into a musical for Broadway, which went on to win eight Tony awards. Finally, the creative team behind *Once* took the musical to Ireland, England, Australia and Korea.

Contemporary Experimentation: The Sawdust Approach

Gary Vaynerchuk (b. 1975) is an entrepreneur, investor, public speaker and social media expert. An energetic man from Belarus in the former USSR, he lives in Queens, New York, with his family.

Vaynerchuk has built multiple businesses including his family's wine business and more recently the digital marketing agency Vaynermedia.

He's also the author of four books and is a master of creating content to promote his businesses and his ideas in the form of articles, video clips, infographics, social media updates, for podcast and YouTube episodes.

Although Vaynerchuk has an entire team behind him today, for years he created his content almost entirely by himself. The volume and intensity of Vaynerchuk's work would exhaust a reasonable man or woman.

So how did Vaynerchuk do it? Is he superhuman?

The mogul says, "It was just me doing my thing."

He excels at taking a single great idea and transforming it repeatedly for different platforms. In an opening to one recent blog post, Vaynerchuk wrote,

> I'm about to get real meta on you: the article you're about to read was made from a video, that was made from the making of an article, that was originally based off a video."

When Vaynerchuk is launching a book, he creates content around the book that informs his YouTube show, podcast, blog posts and social media updates. The ideas don't vary much from one medium to the next. Instead, the creative master tailors his language and how he presents his ideas for each platform and audience.

Vaynerchuk's experimentation with form and substance enables him to reach different audiences in different places without running out of resources, energy or time. He likens this approach to figuring out his sawdust, saying,

> It's the byproducts of your output whether you're a podcaster or a writer or entrepreneur. It's someone who took the sawdust after cutting a bunch of 2x4s, repackaging it and then selling it."

Vaynerchuk recommends that entrepreneurs, marketers,

writers, artists and anyone with an idea to share, repurpose (or change the form of) their work as much as possible because this is the best way to reach a wider audience.

 Create content around the topics in your book, and make sure that content brings value to the consumers you most want to target. You'll create buzz around your brand and book, and people will see that you know what you're talking about. Then they'll only want to buy your book more, right?"

Several years ago, I was employed as a content marketer for a software company. It was my job to write articles and blog posts and transform these into ebooks, infographics, social media posts and more.

At first, I was uncomfortable with this way of working. It felt lazy and uninspired. (Sorry Vaynerchuk). I liked the idea of sitting down to a blank canvas or a blank screen every time and coming up with something new, something better.

But I quickly discovered when you're up against a deadline, and you've got a tight budget, reinventing the wheel every time isn't possible.

Even if you have lots of resources, you're doing your audience a disservice if you haven't tried to get your ideas in front of as many people as possible.

If someone reads a blog post, that doesn't mean they'll download an ebook, just as a podcast listener isn't always the same person as a YouTube viewer (or a musical fan isn't necessarily a film buff).

So, with the help of a graphic designer, I turned chapters and key findings from an ebook into an eye-catching infographic and social media updates. And in doing so we were able to reach more people.

Now, here's a secret about this book:

Some of the chapters you're reading started life as blog posts, which I later reworked, polished and turned into writing that's more appropriate for a book than a blog. Rewriting these posts as book chapters helped me think them through a little deeper and it's a fantastic way to squeeze more life from an idea.

Whether you're a writer, musician or artist, examine what you've already created. Then consider who hasn't discovered your work and figure out if you can change the form of your ideas, if you can repackage your sawdust and serve a new audience. Because ideas that matter transcend traditional forms of expression.

Form and Music

Passing through the doors of the Hermitage Museum, a bolt of pain shot across my temple, and my stomach lurched. I'd been up till 3:00 a.m. the night before with four friends drinking Platinka vodka and eating black caviar in a traditional St. Petersburg restaurant.

Having only four days to see Russia, we rose early after our boozy night out, walked down the bank of the Volga River and into the Hermitage. But I lacked the energy or willpower to spend the rest of the day browsing the sights in one of the world's largest and oldest museums.

I trudged from one room of this former Russian palace to the next sipping a bottle of sparkling water, until finally, I reached the Hercules Room. When I saw what was in there, I forgot about my hangover.

Matisse's *Dance* and *La Musique* hung side-by-side on one of the red walls, apart from the rest of the masterpieces.

Dance is a canvas painting of five naked men and women who look like folk figures from a fairy tale. They're pulling each other and dancing around in a violent circle on top of a green hill holding hands.

In *La Musique*, two of the five folk figures are playing the violin and pipe while the others are sitting on the grass, their hands on their knees, their black eyes, red ears, and mouths opening as the music plays.

In both paintings, the robust dark reds, greens and blues come alive, and when you look at these men and women long enough, they seem to shine, to move, to dance.

It's as if Matisse is still playing music for us some sixty years after his death using his paintbrush.

On my way out of the museum, I bought a print of *La Musique* and when I got home I framed it and hung it on the wall next to where I write.

When I'm stuck, feel uninspired, and my bucket runs empty, I look at Matisse's work to remind myself what's possible through experimenting with form and substance.

Creative Takeaways

- Pick one of your most recent creative projects. Select an idea and experiment with it.
- Repackage your successful ideas into different forms and serve different audiences.

4

CHANGE YOUR PERSPECTIVE

"After all these years, I have come to realise that I must go through a period of agony and torture before I have a breakthrough."
– Hans Zimmer

"Where are you going next?"

I was sick of this question.

I was nearly two months into a summer backpacking trip around Brazil, and I'd begun to loathe the backpackers around me. They kept asking me questions – not because they cared about my answer, but so they could prove their experiences were more valid – and I was tired of it.

I guess I was jealous.

I was searching for an answer that didn't sound cliché, so when a crusty backpacker suggested the Pantanal I jumped at the chance of an experience far from the beaten track.

The world's largest swampland, the Pantanal is located

mostly in Brazil, just below the Amazon jungle. To get there, I travelled on a bus for 12 hours in a cramped seat by a leaky toilet, and me with a wide grin that said, "This is roughing it."

Arriving at camp, I was struck by the novel soundtrack of the Pantanal: a cacophony of chattering monkeys and birds chirping in the trees and the rustle of bats flying overhead.

Our guide, Nikola, was a stocky man with bloodshot eyes and a series of scars around one of his forearms.

He flashed his torch onto the ground and said:

"Don't go to the toilet cubicle without a torch."

I couldn't see much more than a metre in front of me, and when I looked down, I was shocked by the mass of ants swirling over my feet.

At breakfast the next morning, we swatted flies from our watermelons and pineapples and then started what turned out to be a seven-hour trek through the forest and savannah land. Nikola dismissed our attempts at small talk with a grunt or a nod.

Still, his perception of the landscape was unlike ours. I'd see a mark in the sand or walk past a bush rustling and think nothing of it until Nikola explained the mark in the sand was a snake trail and that there was a monkey inside the bush.

Later, a group of lemurs charged across our path – their yellow and black tails bouncing in the air like a sea of frustrated hairballs.

That afternoon, we went horseback riding.

I lagged behind the rest of the group. Every time I tried to direct the horse, it trotted the other way.

I was grateful when Nikola swapped his horse with

mine. Five minutes later, the same protesting horse reared in the air and flung our guide to the ground.

Nikola jumped up, grabbed the horse by the reins, smacked it in the face and stared into its eyes. The animal went quiet, and Nikola climbed back into the saddle. Then our horses rode us back to camp, breaking into a gallop as we drew near.

That night, a skinny man with a pockmarked face pulled an anaconda from the inside of a tree. He held it in the air and then, perhaps because I was standing closest, he thrust the wriggling snake into my hands.

He grinned at my shocked expression.

"Put it back in the tree," he said "Good luck."

I could feel the raw power of the animal pulsing through my arms.

After my friends had taken a photo, I dropped the snake onto the ground and walked off, very quickly.

Over a local sour drink, I asked our guide Nikola about the scars on his forearm.

He waved the aforementioned hand.

"Puma."

In broken English, Nikola confessed he dreamt of travelling on the Orient Express one day. But he explained he hadn't left the camp in more than six months. It was his home and his work.

His dreams for his future were being shaped by his day-to-day experiences in the Pantanal just as mine were shaped by my mundane experiences at home in Ireland.

Early the next morning, we went fishing for piranhas. Nikola explained piranha also means "slut" because "they will eat anything."

Much later, I read online that only certain breeds attack humans, and even those breeds are attracted only to blood.

Then, a friend pointed out to what looked like an alligator at the edge of the lake.

"They are more afraid of us than you are of them."

Nikola proceeded to skin a piranha and toss the remains into a snapping alligator's mouth.

That night, we ate barbecued fish and boiled rice.

After dinner, Nikola asked us to shine our torches onto a lake at the back of the camp. Dozens of red eyes were gliding soundlessly through the water and away from the light.

Looking at those alligators, my belly full of piranhas, it was hard not to feel pleased about this different view of the world.

While I took photos, Nikola stood to the side and looked at his watch. The absurdity of eating piranhas (they were bland and boney) and watching alligators was an alien experience from anything I'd done at home in Ireland, but Nikola had seen all this, many times.

The Unique Perspective of an Outsider

German composer Hans Zimmer (b. 1957) spent much of his spare time as a child and teenager composing music and playing with synthesisers.

As a young man, he played in clubs and bars with up-and-coming pop bands and composed jingles for a BBC mini-series broadcast in the UK.

In the late 1980s, director Barry Levinson hired Zimmer to compose a soundtrack for his film *Rain Man*. Although this was Zimmer's big break, he was still an outsider. He felt afraid that he didn't know what he was doing and that his creative peers would expose him.

Instead, Zimmer was surprised to find Hollywood musicians were using technology that was years behind what he had used in Europe. In many cases, the directors only heard a score for the first time when the entire orchestra had assembled.

Zimmer saw this as an incredibly unproductive way to compose music, so he used his experiences as a European composer to play a score for Levinson on a computer.

"Instead of making him imagine what the French horns would sound like, I'd bring them in on a computer," Zimmer told Gillian Segal in the book *Getting There*.

Rain Man won an Oscar for best picture, and Zimmer received a nomination for best soundtrack. Subsequently, he composed iconic soundtracks for films like *Driving Miss Daisy* and the *Pirates of the Caribbean* series. He also won an Oscar for composing the soundtrack for *The Lion King*.

Zimmer found creative success in a way his peers couldn't because he was an expert and because he possessed the unique perspective of an outsider, but even a master of Zimmer's talents would face many challenges.

In the late 2000s, Christopher Nolan hired Zimmer to compose the soundtrack for *The Dark Knight* series. The second film in this series is a particularly dark thriller, and Zimmer (always in search of a novel idea) wanted to compose music "that people would truly hate."

During his search for this distinctive sound, Zimmer composed 90,000 bars of experimental music. One of his more absurd ideas involved striking razor blades against piano strings to get the haunting melody he was looking for.

Even then, Zimmer was unhappy with the results,

 On the last day of recording with a one-hundred-person orchestra, I found myself lying on the couch in the back of the room experiencing terrible chest pains. I hadn't slept in weeks and was thinking, I'm going to die. But I didn't say anything. Chris Nolan, the director, who knows me very well, saw that I was in serious trouble. He walked over to the microphone and announced to the musicians, "I think we've recorded enough. You can all go home." I sat up and said, "No, no, no, no! We haven't!" Chris repeated, "I think we've recorded enough." And, of course, he was right."

German philosopher Arthur Schopenhauer (1788-1860) investigated the purpose of music extensively in his essays and writings. He argued great music helps the artist and listener understand the essence of our reality and the striving that underlies and unifies the universe.

In Zimmer's case, he was searching for a dark reality, which might go some way to explaining his creative struggles. Eventually, Zimmer found a more relevant sound by settling on a single note played on the cello by his colleague, Martin Tillman. After listening to the final soundtrack, director Nolan said exploring it was "a pretty unpleasant experience."

Zimmer was delighted; this was his intention and his iconic soundtrack was nominated for an Oscar. Today, Zimmer is an accomplished composer whom Hollywood directors and producers seek out, but he still believes he must go through "a period of agony and torture" before achieving a breakthrough.

For him, the river is a dark place.

Despite his creative setbacks, Zimmer pushes himself to avoid fixed ways of thinking, and he advises new artists who want to do the same to try something new every day.

Karl Duncker would agree.

The Curious Case of Duncker's Candle

German psychologist Karl Duncker (1903-1940) developed a problem-solving challenge known as *Duncker's Candle Problem*, which was published posthumously in 1945.

He presented participants with a table propped against a wall, on top of which were a packet of matches, a box of thumbtacks and a candle. He then asked participants to attach the candle to the wall and prevent any wax from dripping from the candle onto the table below.

If you're thinking about a solution to this creative problem, you've got five minutes.

The first time I faced *Duncker's Candle Problem*, I decided the answer lay in attaching the candle to the wall using the tacks.

Like many students' answers, my solution felt perfectly reasonable, and it was perfectly wrong. Pressing thumbtacks into a waxy candle is messy and inefficient. I also came across other answers where students decided to melt the candle and use the hot wax to attach it to the wall.

So what's wrong with all of these solutions?

Well, they're overly complicated, and they rely on a fixed view of the world.

Instead, all you have to do is pick up the box of thumbtacks and empty the thumbtacks onto the table. Now, use a single thumbtack to attach the box to the wall, and then put the candle into the box.

Simple, isn't it?

Duncker's Candle Problem reveals many of us are attached to rigid definitions of what's possible and impossible.

We fail to see the box as a separate object that we can use to solve the problem. We're afraid of breaking the rules and doing things in abnormal or absurd ways. In the end, because of our fixed perspective, the quality of our ideas suffers.

The good news is you can find practical and novel ideas if you know where to start and if you're prepared to leave common sense behind (if only for a little while).

From the Absurd to the Relevant

How can you find an idea that's novel and useful, as Zimmer did with *The Dark Knight* soundtrack?

Well, I'd like you to think of your creative project as a mountain. At the top of this mountain, you can mine bizarre, outlandish and absurd ideas, and at the bottom of the mountain you can extract practical, relevant and logical ideas.

You're not looking to set up camp at the top of this mountain because the conditions up there are too inhospitable for your ideas to thrive. There's also little point in settling at the bottom of this mountain because basecamp is a crowded place; we've all been there.

Instead, there's a hidden place between the points of absurdity and relevancy that is rich in novel, yet useful ideas. Think of it as a secret forge where you can combine the novelty of the absurd with the applicability of the practical. Here, your inner genius can get to work and smelt the golden ideas you crave.

The question is, "How can you get to this secret forge while expending a minimal amount of your limited creative resources?"

From absurd to relevant ideas

Create a Thought Experiment

If a teacher, friend, family member or colleague has ever said, "You live inside your head," you'll recognise this as a perplexing and sometimes embarrassing experience.

I know because this happens to me regularly, but the next time someone criticises you for this behaviour, tell them you're engaging in a thought experiment, that you're thinking your ideas through just like Albert Einstein (1879-1955).

They'll probably look at you like you're crazy, but here's the thing: Your imagination will help you get to the top of the mountain to mine your absurd ideas.

Just like Albert Einstein.

He lived in his head for hours at a time, where he conducted thought experiments or *gedankenexperimente*. During these exercises, he took an idea or a scenario and spun it around in his mind.

As a young schoolchild in Aarau in Switzerland, Einstein attempted to picture riding alongside a light beam. He said,

 In Aarau I made my first rather childish experiments in thinking that had a direct bearing on the Special Theory. If a person could run after a light wave with the same speed as light, you would have a wave arrangement which could be completely independent of time. Of course, such a thing is impossible."

It's easy to imagine Einstein's teacher telling him to stop daydreaming and pay attention to the lesson in front of him.

Einstein later credited this thought experiment as the starting point for his *Theory of Relativity*. During his late twenties and early thirties, he used mathematical equations and the rigour of science to take his absurd idea and formulate an applicable theory.

Some of Einstein's other thought experiments involved

lightning strikes, falling painters, moving trains and even imagining the velocity of electrons.

While Einstein gave time to daydreams and his imagination, he eventually uprooted ideas from the recesses of his mind, wrote them down, worked on them and published his findings.

In other words, he climbed down from his absurd daydreams about running after light or imagining the speed of an electron and turned his thoughts into practical scientific concepts.

The Practical and Absurd Creative Mind

The next time you're struggling with a creative project, try to come up with as many absurd ideas as possible.

Like I recommended with freewriting in an earlier chapter, push past your point of comfort and cognitive biases and have fun with your ideas, fantasies and daydreams. Strike razor blades against the piano string, if you will.

Let's say I want to come up with a creative way of promoting a new novel. Here are three absurd promotional ideas:

- Hire a plane to paint the book title in the sky over crowds at Wembley football stadium.
- Tattoo the title of the book to my face.
- Stand naked on O'Connell Street in Dublin City Centre while reading my book out loud and streaming said recording on Facebook.

Once you have these absurd ideas, work your way down to what's relevant – move from razor blades towards the cello playing a single note. The climb down is always easier.

In the case of the above example, here's what I came up with:

- Give away 500 copies of the book to bloggers, would-be readers and reviewers and offer one of their readers a holiday.
- Mock up a photograph of me with this tattoo in Photoshop and use this for a Facebook advertising campaign.
- Record myself reading my book out loud at locations featured in the book (standing on the Giant's Causeway, on a boat to the Aran Islands etc.) around Ireland and upload these recordings to YouTube.

James Altucher (b. 1968) is a successful self-published author who is adept at book promotions and someone who moves from the absurd to the relevant with ease.

Altucher didn't tattoo the title of his best-selling self-published book *Choose Yourself* to his face. Instead, he made a T-shirt with every word from his book printed on it and then proceeded to give away these T-shirts to would-be readers and reviewers.

Remember, it's OK to explore hunches, probe new avenues of thought and bring back anything unusual or odd that you find. Later on, sift through these discoveries and figure out what's usable and what to put aside. Your creative ideas are never wrong, not even the absurd ones.

Creative masters like Zimmer and Einstein change their perspectives as often as they can because even the novel and fresh become . . .

Old and Stale

On the last day of my trip to the Pantanal, Nikola woke us before dawn. The sun stepped lazily onto the horizon and light trickled down across the fields.

It was a beautiful Brazilian morning, but I was tired of the chirping birds and monkeys, the bats flying overhead at night, of being bitten by ants, slapping mosquitos from my arms and my tongue turning numb from the taste of repellant.

I'd had enough of the Pantanal, the early mornings, the uncomfortable heat and using a torch to go to the toilet. The camp felt old, fixed and confining.

We watched the sun light up the dirt track leading to the camp. A jeep was bringing a new group of backpackers towards us. My off-the-beaten-track experience felt unique compared only to where I'd been before and where I was going next.

I thought of Rio de Janeiro and about football, sex and religion. Change was coming, and I relished it.

I didn't think much about the Pantanal again until months later back in Ireland. There, during grey days in the office park where I worked, I wondered if Nikola was still fantasising about the Orient Express while leading tourists around the savannahs and forests.

I fought with the photocopier and imagined what would happen if we were attacked by pumas at 3:37 p.m. on a random Tuesday. A colleague, seeing me lost in thought, asked what I was thinking about.

When I told her, she said, "That's absurd."

Creative Takeaways

- Set time aside to daydream and for thought experiments.
- Write down 100 ideas. They should be as extreme and as absurd as possible. Now climb down from these ideas to what's relevant.

5

EMBRACE CONSTRAINTS OF TIME AND MONEY

"Don't give me any money, don't give me any people, but give freedom, and I'll give you a movie that looks gigantic."
– Robert Rodriguez

An accomplished tailor once told me he listens to what his customers want before showing them three suits.

"Why three suits?" I asked.

"I never give a customer too much choice," he said. "The customer will just find it harder to come to a decision."

This tailor understands that the human brain dislikes too many choices whereas constraints simplify decision-making.

So how does this apply to your creative work?

Well, have you ever heard someone say:

"If only I had more money, then I could do it."

Or

"I don't have time to paint today."

Or

"I don't have time to write today."

Many aspiring creative people come out with things like this when the time comes to write, paint, play or draw.

The harsh truth is these people are making excuses.

If you want to become more creative, you must recognise you don't need more resources, time or energy. These things are not your friends. They lead to bloat and excess.

Working on an idea is often more about problem solving than it is about having a bright white canvas before you and unlimited resources at your disposal.

Instead of being concerned about what you lack, you can use constraints of time, money and resources as a float to guide you down the river, as a means of becoming *more creative*, just like accomplished photographers, film-makers and musicians have done.

Turning What You Lack into a Creative Asset

One of ten children, Texas-born Robert Rodriguez (b. 1968) wanted to become a filmmaker just like John Carpenter. His earliest memories are of going to an old movie theatre in San Antonio, Texas, to watch classic films like *Escape from New York*.

Rodriguez created amateur home movies with a JVC video cassette recorder while he was a boy, but when he enrolled at the University of Texas in 1991, he discovered his dream profession had a costly barrier to entry.

Rodriguez had an idea for an action film about a musician set in Mexico. Lacking the money to realise his vision, he enrolled as a paid subject in a clinical experiment at a drug research facility. He used the $7,000 paycheque from these tests to pay the cost of shooting his debut film *El Mariachi*.

Because he had so little money, Rodriguez embraced constraints as a way of becoming *more* creative.

To reduce expenses, Rodriguez didn't hire a film crew, he took on many of the roles himself, and he encouraged the few actors in the movie to help with behind-the-scenes work. Instead of setting up sound recording equipment, Rodriguez shot in silence and dubbed the audio in post-production.

Rodriguez even froze the action every few seconds and changed the camera angle to give the film the appearance of having multiple cameras. And instead of buying squibs for the shootout scenes, he used condoms filled with fake blood fixed over weightlifting belts.

While describing his barebones approach to film-making in his book *Rebel Without a Crew*, he tells aspiring filmmakers,

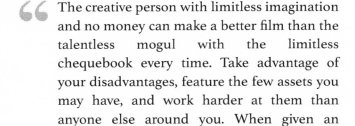

The creative person with limitless imagination and no money can make a better film than the talentless mogul with the limitless chequebook every time. Take advantage of your disadvantages, feature the few assets you may have, and work harder at them than anyone else around you. When given an opportunity, deliver excellence and never quit."

Rodriguez originally meant for *El Mariachi* to be released to the Mexican home video market, but film executives at Columbia Pictures were so impressed with his achievements on a budget that they bought the distribution rights and helped Rodriguez market the movie.

El Mariachi went on to win multiple international awards

and spawned two sequels, *Desperado* and *Once Upon a Time in Mexico*. In 2011, *El Mariachi* was selected for preservation in the United States' National Film Registry.

Today Rodriguez is an accomplished director, producer, screenwriter, editor and musician. He is also the man behind film franchises like *Spy Kids* and the *Mexico* trilogy.

Even though Rodriguez has more financial and creative freedom today, he goes out of his way to impose artificial constraints upon all of his creative projects.

He recently said, "I want all of my movies to not have enough money, to not have enough time, so we are forced to be more creative."

The Freedom of Restrictions

Irish singer-songwriter Damien Rice (b. 1973) is another creative master who sometimes uses a lack of resources to accomplish more.

In 1998, Rice was the front-man for the Irish band Juniper. They'd signed a six-album record deal with Poly-Gram and their two singles, "Weatherman" and "World is Dead", were a critical and commercial success in Ireland.

So when Rice quit the band to travel across Italy and busk around Europe, Juniper's fans were shocked.

Both Rice and I attended secondary school Salesian College in Celbridge County Kildare, although he was several years ahead of me. In 2000, I interviewed Rice for the school paper, and I asked him why he quit on success.

Rice explained he disliked creating radio-friendly music.

"And where do you see yourself in ten years?" I asked.

"It's not where I see myself going," he said. "It's who I see myself as."

I was struck by Rice's intense approach to his art.

He still wanted to record music, but he lacked the resources of a band, having other people to rely on and most importantly of all, a major label record deal.

Between 1998 and 2002, Rice wrote and composed all the tracks on what would become *O* on a shoestring budget.

His track "Older Chests", for example, features a sample of cars passing by and the laughter of a group of school children on the street. Rice couldn't afford to hire kids to come into the studio, and he didn't hire a producer to create this sound for him.

Instead, Rice took his microphone and recorder, stood at the gates of a primary school in Celbridge, and recorded the chatter of children as they finished school for the day. The result is something more natural and authentic sounding than a studio recording.

When he released *O* in 2002, it became a success in Ireland, the United Kingdom and the United States thanks to songs like "Volcano" and "The Blower's Daughter".

Rice did what he did in a pre-smartphone, pre-YouTube world. He used his lack of money and recognition to ground his work. Some years later I stumbled across an interview with Rice where he said,

 A kite needs to be tied down in order to fly. I learned how important restrictions can sometimes be in order to experience freedom."

Today, it's much easier for musicians to create on a shoestring budget and get their music out into the world. You can use restrictions and creative limitations (like lacking a record deal or having the resources of a studio) to lend an

authenticity, a freshness and a sense of urgency to your work that isn't possible when you're successful.

Instead of ruminating about what you need, your lack of resources can help you ground a project and learn more about the creative process.

Getting Your Technique Down

New York-man Robert Mapplethorpe (1946-1989) wanted to do one thing with his life: to live for art. During his teens and early twenties, he experimented with drawing, painting and sculpture.

Then, in 1970 a friend loaned Mapplethorpe a 360 Land camera, a clunky, but technically simple, silver and black device. He settled on the camera as his creative tool of expression because "it was more honest."

At first, Mapplethorpe restricted himself to taking pictures only of his former girlfriend and lifelong creative partner singer Patti Smith. The confines of a single muse shaped his creative vision and enabled him to hone his technique. In *Just Kids*, Patti wrote,

 He was comfortable with me and he needed time to get his technique down. The mechanics of the camera were simple, but the options were limited."

That wasn't the only restriction Mapplethorpe faced. In the 1970s, camera film was expensive, and he couldn't afford the liberty of mistakes. So he made every shot count.

Mapplethorpe developed his technique and visual eye with the 360 Land Camera and later a Polaroid. In 1973, he held his first solo photography exhibition at the Light Gallery in New York.

With success came more financial and creative resources. A patron bought Mapplethorpe an expensive Hasselblad camera (a type of camera previously used to photograph the moon landings).

Although a professional-grade camera gave Mapplethorpe more choices and control over his use of light, he didn't learn anything about the creative process from having access to more powerful tools.

According to Smith, "Robert had already defined his visual vocabulary. The new camera taught him nothing, just allowed him to get exactly what he was looking for.

Mapplethorpe wanted to document New York's S&M scene, and his subsequent exhibition shocked audiences, but impressed his peers. He said,

> I don't like that particular word 'shocking.' I'm looking for the unexpected. I'm looking for things I've never seen before...I was in a position to take those pictures. I felt an obligation to do them."

Mapplethorpe went on to photograph a series of male and female nudes, delicate flower still lifes and portraits of artists and celebrities. He also collaborated intensely with the world's first female bodybuilder Lisa Lyon.

He continued to push photography forwards as an art form until he died of AIDS in 1989.

Today, Mapplethorpe is regarded as one of the twentieth century's most provocative visual artists, and his work is displayed in galleries around the United States, South America and Europe.

Working Around the Margins of the Day

In 2013, after several difficult months out of work, I started a full-time job in a profession that I wasn't entirely comfortable with.

Before I started this job, I set out to write my first nonfiction book *A Handbook for the Productive Writer*. As my day job took over, I found I didn't have much time or energy in the evenings to write my book. I wrote less and less each day until finally, my progress ground to a frustrating halt.

I told myself it was OK to push out publishing this book because nobody was breathing down my neck looking for a first draft.

Besides, I'd just started a new job. *I should go easier on myself.*

As the weeks went by, this felt more like an excuse and less like a genuine reason for not writing my book.

Then, I read James Altucher's *Choose Yourself.*

He lays out a bold case for why creative people need to consider themselves entrepreneurs in charge of their destiny.

Altucher believes if we don't take charge of our creative lives, no one else will. We must choose ourselves. He wrote,

> The key slogan is, "Keep failing until you accidentally no longer fail." That's persistence."

Was I just making excuses? Was I a mediocre entrepreneur? Was I just another failed writer? I looked in the mirror and said, "Yes, yes, and yes."

I knew then something had to change.

I didn't know what to do until I read about "Parkinson's

Law". British historian and author Cyril Northcote Parkinson put forward the argument in the 1950s that "work expands so as to fill the time available for completion." It's since been applied to many other fields, including the arts.

In other words, even if I had all day to write, it still wouldn't feel like enough time.

So I faced a crucial decision.

I could either put off writing my book until I settled into my new job and had some free time. Or I could use my lack of time as a boundary for my work and commit to writing the first draft, even if it meant getting up an hour or two before work and giving up television, computer games and other passive leisure activities in the evening.

I chose the latter and while the first few weeks were hard, writing around the margins of the day forced me to work faster.

Some of my sentences weren't as tight as they could have been, and some of my arguments needed fleshing out. But like a runner who stumbles over a pothole in the road and keeps going, I didn't stop to fix each mistake because I didn't have time (at least during the first draft).

Thanks to my self-imposed deadline, I turned around an admittedly rough first draft within a month or two, which I then spent another two months editing and polishing.

When the time came to self-publish the book, I was as busy in work as I ever was. I realised if I'd put off writing the book and hadn't used constraints, I would never have finished it.

I'd like to tell you the book was a critical and commercial success.

It wasn't, but when I self-published the book, I didn't care about my lack of obvious success. I discovered I was the kind of person who could take an idea, work it out and finish it; and even if I never sold a copy, I'd accomplished a small, personal victory within a more public failure.

Over the next few weeks and for the first time in my life I received emails from readers who told me things like,

"I was pleasantly surprised at how Bryan Collins's *A Handbook for the Productive Writer* lives up to its promise.

As the author of over 40 books and thousands of articles and blog posts, numerous ideas resonated with my experiences, but even more important, there were numerous hacks and suggestions that were new to me.

Bryan's writing engages you from the start, yet he doesn't waste a word. Topics are concisely covered with admirable detail and momentum. An excellent guide for both new writers and those in need of a quick recharge."

I also received more critical reviews like this:

"This book has a lot of good content especially for the beginning writer. I will definitely put some of his suggestions into action. But . . . wading through all of the mistakes makes this a difficult read."

I won't lie; the critical reviews were hard to take. After I read this one, I hired another editor to help me fix these mistakes before relaunching the book. Then, I stopped writing it and moved on with my life.

Establishing a boundary around my work helped me write, finish and ship it and taught me more about the act of writing.

While the book isn't perfect, finishing it and getting real-world feedback from readers – *living, breathing readers* – was motivating enough to drive me to start and finish a second (and better) book.

The Power of Constraint

Limitations aren't confining; they're liberating.

Creative masters like Mapplethorpe saw chaos around them and brought order to it. What better way to bring order than to restrict yourself to a few chosen tools, a big idea or means of expression?

If you were told you could write, draw, film or paint anything you liked using any material imaginable, you would have difficulty knowing where to start.

On the other hand, if you were given a creative brief that required you to write 1,000 words about the importance of storytelling or sketch Dublin at dawn using charcoal, these restrictions would force your brain to come up with more inspired ideas.

You can overcome creative overwhelm by narrowing your choices.

For example, if you don't have the freedom to work on your ideas for eight hours straight because you have a job or other personal commitments, use the constraint of time to create what's most important to you first thing in the morning or at night.

Don't be afraid of a looming deadline; use it as a catalyst to drive yourself and your project forwards.

Or if you lack the financial resources to conclude your project, reduce, remove and simplify your work and then finish what you can afford.

You can always come back to the unfinished parts of your creative project later on. An idea that matters doesn't demand a million dollar budget and five years of development.

Creative masters like Rodriguez, Rice and Mapplethorpe imposed constraints on their works rather than seeking out unlimited resources. These constraints helped them learn more about the creative process.

When you have too much freedom, getting started or finishing your work can feel impossible. On the other hand, artificially imposed constraints will help you come up with better ideas and give you an end goal to work towards.

It will narrow your creative vision and help you focus on what's important.

Creative Takeaways

- Do you lack enough time or money to finish your creative project? Use your lack of resources to narrow the scope of your project.
- Don't worry about lacking resources, time or money. These constraints can help you place necessary confines around your projects.

6

BECOME AN HONOURABLE THIEF

"Immature poets imitate; mature poets steal; bad poets deface what they take, and good poets make it into something better, or at least something different."
– T.S. Eliot

Twyla Tharp has a secret weapon.

There is nothing particularly mystical, secretive or expensive about her weapon. It's a simple cardboard box from Home Depot, but Twyla has won many creative victories with it.

In the summer of 2000, Twyla Tharp (b. 1941) invited the artist Billy Joel to her home in Manhattan. There, she showed Joel the first item from her box: a twenty-minute videotape of dancing to his compositions, like "Uptown Girl" and "Big Shot".

After seeing the video, Joel told Tharp, "I didn't know my stuff could look so good."

Feeling encouraged, she took two blue index cards from

the box for Joel to see. On the first index card, she'd written, "Tell a story," and on the second she'd written, "Make dance pay."

Joel wanted to know more, so Twyla pitched her vision for a Broadway musical called *Movin' Out*. She envisioned composing and choreographing a dance show set to 27 Billy Joel songs.

Tharp's dance show would depict the lives of five Long Island kids from 1965 to 1984, set to the backdrop of the Vietnam War.

Joel agreed to her big idea.

As a composer and dancer with more than 40 years of experience, Tharp has choreographed dozens of award-winning ballet shows, and she has worked on numerous films and TV shows including *Hair* and *The Golden Section*.

Over the next few months, Tharp added to her cardboard box of ideas.

She included Joel's CDs, the opening line of Homer's *Illiad*, tapes of the singer's live performances and his lectures. She also added television and radio footage from the Vietnam War and movies such as *The Deer Hunter* and *Full Metal Jacket*.

Tharp also included Michael Herr's *Dispatches* as well other books from that period. She added notebooks of little ideas, photos of Joel from the 1970s and song lists. Tharp even placed show notes for her music director inside the box.

Movin' Out premiered in 2002. It won two Tony awards and became an international success.

Tharp fills a box with ideas like this for almost every creative project.

On the front of each box, Tharp writes the name of her creative project. She fills the boxes with newspaper clippings, CDs, notebooks, pictures, pieces of art, and record-ings of her dancing. She organises for her shows by gathering ideas from books, films, music and shows and reflecting on what she finds.

Even if Tharp doesn't know what her big idea is about or where she's going, the act of filling a box helps her commit to a big idea.

The box inspires the choreographer and fuels fresh thinking for her shows. The filling of a box is a creative ritual that protects her from forgetting a good idea or feeling uninspired.

In *The Creative Habit*, Tharp explains,

> The box makes me feel connected to a project. It is my soil. I feel this even when I've back-burnered a project: I may have put the box away on a shelf, but I know it's there. The project name on the box in bold black lettering is a constant reminder that I had an idea once and may come back to it very soon."

Tharp is a creative master who knows where to look for ideas, and she looks everywhere. She looks to the wider world, the work of her contemporaries and even to her past success.

Sometimes after a show ends, Tharp takes an old box from storage and goes through her old ideas to see what inspired her and to trace the roots of her creative projects. Tharp believes old ideas sometimes suggest new ones.

> For me, personally, a successful piece is a piece that suggests the next one – that put me in a place where I have the energy and the

vision to move forward and tackle a whole other approach to something."

Like Tharp, keep a box and fill it with what inspires you. It doesn't have to be a physical cardboard box either. Use a notebook, a scratchpad, a Dictaphone, a journal, your computer or whatever works. Don't obsess about the box or your research process because to do so is to procrastinate.

The river doesn't care what you bring down to the bank. Your creative tool is less important than having a place where you put ideas from books you read, art you admire, films you watch, museums you visit, music you listen to, the conversations you share and even from your dreams.

Once these ideas are safe, review what you have and search for common themes, as Tharp did when she went through her cardboard box of ideas and discovered Vietnam as the theme that would unite the characters in her Joel musical.

Once you cultivate a habit of gathering ideas and working through your findings, you'll be able to combine these old ideas in new and exciting ways.

What Steve Jobs Did

Steve Jobs (1955-2011) was a creative master who knew what he wanted, and in 1979 he wanted to see what was inside the Xerox PARC.

The Xerox research centre in Palo Alto had become a place for technologists and top computer scientists like Alan Kay to research big ideas and work without interruption.

At that time, using a computer was a daunting affair. The touchscreens and point and click systems we take for granted today didn't exist. Instead, computer users typed relatively complicated commands into an expensive and far from intuitive computer.

Kay famously said, "The best way to predict the future is to invent it."

Along with his team at Xerox PARC, he wanted to make computers more accessible to the general public and particularly for small children.

To realise their dream, a team at Xerox PARC invented a user-friendly graphical interface for a small personal computer, known as a DynaBook.

In a precursor to today's Windows and Mac operating systems, the screen of their computer had documents and folders on it, and users controlled the DynaBook using a point and click device instead of typing cumbersome commands.

While Kay's team worked on their big idea, Xerox's venture capital division was negotiating the details of a $1 million dollar investment in Apple.

In 1979, Apple was one of Silicon Valley's most attractive new technology companies and a year away from its initial public offering (IPO).

The Apple management team accepted Xerox's investment on the condition that they show Jobs and his engineering team what was going on inside Xerox PARC. At the time, Xerox believed it was getting the better bargain.

They were wrong.

When Jobs and his engineering team saw the graphical interface under development inside Xerox PARC, they couldn't believe how far the technology had advanced. Jobs later told his biographer Walter Isaacson,

 It was like a veil being lifted from my eyes. I

could see what the future of computing was destined to be."

Xerox's three-button mouse included with the Dyna-Book cost $300 to build. The computer itself retailed for an eye-watering sixteen thousand dollars, a sum beyond the means of the average consumer. Jobs immediately set about creating a similar interface, but they constrained themselves with a tight budget.

In just six months, his Apple engineering team adapted PARC's ideas, improved the graphical interface and introduced a number of other cost-saving engineering changes. Jobs's team invented a single-button Apple mouse that cost just $15 to make.

The Apple team also added icons and a menu bar to the graphical interface, as well as an ability to open files and folders by double-clicking with their cheaper Apple mouse. They built on a preexisting idea from Xerox PARC and they created the Macintosh operating system.

Later, the fledgling company released the inexpensive Apple Lisa computer, a machine that the general public could both afford and use. Apple went on to sell millions of Silicon Valley's most famous products.

Years later, Jobs said,

If Xerox had known what it had and had taken advantage of its real opportunities . . . it could have been as big as IBM plus Microsoft plus Xerox combined – and the largest high-technology company in the world."

Today, computer historians point to the Xerox PARC

incident as one of the greatest heists in corporate history, perhaps in part because Jobs famously said,

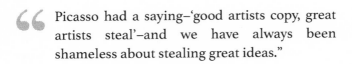

> Picasso had a saying–'good artists copy, great artists steal'–and we have always been shameless about stealing great ideas."

Jobs and his team didn't shamelessly steal a big idea from Xerox PARC and hawk it as their own. Instead, they built on a pre-existing idea that was good but unfinished. Nobody was going to buy a computer that cost $16,000.

Using their business expertise, insight, and knowledge of their customer, Apple solved problems like the Dyna-Book mouse being too expensive and cumbersome to use. They evolved what the team at Xerox PARC started.

Then, Apple did something the team at Xerox PARC failed to do. They shipped a computer that consumers wanted and could afford.

Don't feel too bad for the team at Xerox PARC. Although Xerox withdrew from the personal computer industry altogether, an engineering team at Xerox PARC led by Gary Starkweather went on to invent the laser printer and earn billions for the company.

Jobs did more than steal the ideas of others. He built a career and a company out of gathering old ideas and transforming them into new ones that solved problems for people. Consider what Jobs did when he took to the stage of the Moscone Center in San Francisco in 2007.

It was a pre-touchscreen smartphone world. Most consumers controlled their phones with ugly buttons, listened to their favourite music and accessed the Internet on separate, clunky devices.

Dressed in blue jeans, white trainers and a black turtleneck, Jobs told the world he was going to introduce three revolutionary products: a widescreen iPod with touchscreen controls, a mobile phone and an internet communications device.

He flicked between iOS icons representing these three old ideas. Then, Jobs revealed how Apple had combined these ideas to create the first version of the iPhone.

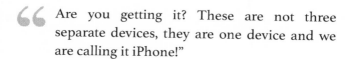 Are you getting it? These are not three separate devices, they are one device and we are calling it iPhone!"

Consumers owned mobile phones, Internet communications devices and portable music players before Jobs's big reveal, but nobody had brought together these technologies.

Like many big ideas, the first iPhone was far from perfect. It lacked many features that mobile phone users now take for granted, such as Bluetooth for connecting to other devices, 3G or 4G for accessing the Internet and the ability to copy and paste text.

Apple offered consumers a powerful (if unfinished) computing device that redefined the mobile phone product category.

They eventually added these missing features to their big idea and transformed the iPhone from a rough and unfinished device into one of the world's most popular pieces of technology.

The story of the iPhone (and the Apple Lisa before it) demonstrates how creative masters like Jobs *gather* preexisting ideas, *combine* them and then *transform* these old ideas into something fresh, into a big idea that people want.

Trace the Path of Your Creative Heroes to Infinity and Beyond

Are you worried about taking other people's ideas? Do you fear this will get you into trouble or that stealing an idea isn't the work of creative people? Or perhaps you don't have Jobs's swagger or Tharp's years of experience?

Francis Ford Coppola (b. 1939), the filmmaker behind films like the *Godfather* and *Apocalypse Now*, offered this advice,

 We want you to take from us. We want you, at first, to steal from us, because you can't steal. You will take what we give you and you will put it in your own voice and that's how you will find your voice. That's how you begin. And then one day someone will steal from you."

The filmmakers at Pixar must have been listening to Coppola when they created Buzz Lightyear. He's a determined and brave space-ranger. As one of the heroes of the Pixar film *Toy Story 2*, he will go to great lengths to protect his friend Woody and the other toys. But even the affable Buzz has a rival.

Throughout *Toy Story 2*, the space ranger is pitted against his nemesis, the evil Emperor Zurg. During the final act, Buzz and the rest of the toys face almost certain defeat at the hands of Zurg.

A moment comes when the emperor is about to defeat Buzz in an elevator shaft, and all looks lost for the toys.

Zurg says, "Surrender Buzz Lightyear. I have won."

Buzz replies, "I'll never give in. You killed my father!"

Emperor Zurg says, "No, Buzz. I *am* your father!"

Before Zurg can defeat Buzz, Rex Dinosaur knocks Zurg off the top of the elevator with his tail, and he falls down the elevator shaft.

This scene mirrors the climax of *Star Wars: The Empire Strikes Back*. In this film, a triumphant Darth Vader defeats Luke Skywalker and cuts off his hand in an epic lightsabre battle.

Then Vader says, "Obi-Wan never told you what happened to your father."

Skywalker replies, "He told me enough! He told me you killed him!"

Vader says, "No, I am your father."

He then asks Skywalker to join him, but the young Jedi throws himself to his apparent death rather than take Vader's side.

Nobody could accuse the *Toy Story 2* filmmakers of stealing unethically from the writers of *Star Wars*. Instead, this climatic *Toy Story 2* scene is one of the funniest moments of the Pixar film because if you know anything about contemporary cinema, you'll appreciate the obvious nod to *Star Wars* and marvel at this humorous retelling of a classic story.

Filmmakers regularly reference artists they look up to, quoting famous lines and pointing to well-known scenes in films they admire. Instead of being angry about what filmmakers do, we breathe in their fresh take on old ideas.

When you do the same, do so with honour. Always hide what you take in plain sight. Tip your hat to the source and provide a way for readers, viewers or listeners of your work to trace the roots of your ideas. Cite your sources if you must.

Standing on the Shoulders of Your Creative Heroes

As an artist, you already have a love for stories, books, films, poetry, art and music, but it's not enough to love art, you must study your chosen medium with the diligence of Tharp and the intensity of Jobs.

When you find writers you admire, study the reference sections of their books and read the work of authors that influenced them.

When you feel the hand of a filmmaker, poet, musician or artist on your shoulder, look deep into their work until you find what keeps them up at night, until you discover what they put inside their cardboard boxes.

Consider what difficult choices the artists overcame while creating their masterworks. Examine the small details of their ideas, pull at the seams and change what you can. Then insert your personal stories and ideas into their works.

Copy what these other artists do, at least at first.

Would you have done things differently? Is there a way you can remix what they created with the voice of another creative expert?

Taking apart another person's work and then putting it back together will help you understand the process behind their big ideas and figure out what inspired them.

Coppola told you to do it. Jobs wants you to do it. Tharp showed you how she did it.

Set time aside to consider art you intensely dislike or feel uncomfortable with too.

Reading a poorly written book, listening to a badly-produced album or watching a clunky film occasionally gives you a frame of reference between what works and what doesn't. It will also help you find your boundaries so you can cross them later on.

Like Jobs, you can improve or combine old ideas or like the Pixar team, you can retell these ideas in new ways.

If you spend time trying to come up with an original idea alone, you won't get very far.

Instead, point to established ideas and explain what they mean to you. Be for or against them, apply them, retell them and transform them.

When you use your voice or tell your story, these old ideas become something else entirely.

They become yours.

Creative Takeaways

- Don't have a box or a file of ideas yet? Write down a list of what inspired you today.
- Pick one writer, artist or creative person whom you admire. Trace their influences as far back as you can go.

7

CULTIVATE INTENSE CURIOSITY

"The desire to know is natural to good men."
– Leonardo da Vinci

When was the last time your ideas got you into trouble?

I love asking difficult questions, but I've learnt hard lessons from other peoples' answers.

Several years ago, I was employed as a care worker in a large service for people with intellectual disabilities. I supported five men and five women in living independent lives in two different houses in a suburb an hour outside of Dublin.

Much of my job involved performing regular household maintenance and hygiene checks around two large bungalows.

I ensured the toilets were clean and the fridges contained enough food to eat. I balanced the houses' financial accounts, paid bills on behalf of the residents and took them shopping for food.

My job included doing all of the things necessary to keep the two houses running just as I would with my own.

The only caveat was that I documented a significant part of what I did every day in various report books, and I also administered medication.

I enjoyed spending time in the company of the residents, but I hated almost everything else about my job. I sometimes had to work overnight shifts for 12 to 24 hours and sleep in a small, cramped bed next to the office desk. Afterwards, I had little energy for anything worthwhile.

I felt as if the unwavering routine, the tedious hygiene checks, and the stifling policies were turning me into an anxious, depressed and prematurely bald man in his early thirties.

One day, my manager called me into the office for a review. These discussions took place every three months, and they served as a means for managers to assess the performance of their team.

I sat on the bed next to the desk.

My manager pulled a large grey folder from the small wooden shelf, slapped it on the table and adjusted her black narrow-frame glasses.

"I'd like you to reread this Bryan." She pushed the grey folder towards me.

I picked up the folder and edged away from her.

The hygiene policy was a heavy grey document. It contained pages and pages about the various household chores we had to complete each day including vacuuming, dusting, cleaning the toilets and so on. It also went into great detail about the tick-charts we had to complete.

I put the policy back on the office desk. "If I spend all day doing these cleaning exercises, how will I have time to take the residents out for coffee or to meet their friends?"

(A big part of the social care profession involves teaching people the independent living skills many of us take for granted.)

"Find time Bryan," she said. "Why is it when you're on shift, the house is never clean enough? You have to make sure there are no crumbs in this toaster. I need you to dust behind the back of the cupboards. We're getting this place ready for a big hygiene inspection, and you're letting the place down."

"Why do we have to do this?" I tried not to look at the tuft of blonde hair on her lip. "Will this feel like a normal home for the men and women who live here if we're going around inspecting the toaster every morning? I don't even engage in this madness in my own house. How will any of *this* teach these men and women the skills they need to succeed in the community?"

My manager held her head and said, "Just for once Bryan, I wish you would stop asking me questions. I didn't make this up. It's the service policy, it's your job, and you need to do it."

"Why should we follow policy blindly?"

"If you have a problem, Bryan why don't you take it up with HR?"

I mumbled something about doing better and walked out of the office.

At the time, I thought I was a model employee because I was speaking up, but I can see now how I complicated life for my manager. She was doing her best to comply with regulations and policies that she had no control over.

Although the work we were doing in the community was important and satisfying (I enjoyed being able to help the men and women live full and independent lives in the community.), I couldn't handle the day-to-day rules and regulations.

It's in my DNA to ask questions and wonder why I should do things one way and not another. It's in my DNA because, after school, I trained for four years as a journalist.

In university, our lecturers rammed home the importance of speaking up to authority, of considering why authority says "This is how we do it", of asking difficult questions.

This interrogative questioning translates to the realm of investigative journalism, but it'll get you in trouble in areas of life. Nobody likes asking or answering difficult questions whether they be about themselves, their work or their ideas.

However, if you want to tap into your inner genius and become more creative, intense curiosity is a skill you must cultivate.

You need to establish whether your big idea is one you should act on or set down because your time and resources are limited.

This is an approach creative masters take.

Why da Vinci Wants You to Cultivate Intense Curiosity

Leonardo da Vinci (1452-1519) was an engineer, chef, writer, artist, inventor, humourist, musician, painter, architect, political advisor, designer, botanist and civil planner.

His most famous paintings include the *Mona Lisa*, *The Last Supper* and *Virgin of the Rocks*. His most famous sculptures include *da Vinci's Horse in Bronze*, and his most famous inventions and drawings include the helicopter and the parachute.

So how did da Vinci achieve so much in 70 years?

While he was a genius, da Vinci cultivated intense

curiosity about everyone he met and everything he came across. He asked difficult questions and used the answers to inform his inventions, ideas and creations.

Da Vinci kept dozens of notebooks and journals throughout his life, many of which still exist. In these, he recorded how he spent days roaming the countryside searching for answers to things he didn't understand.

He wanted to know why shells existed on top of mountains, why lightning is visible immediately, but the sound of thunder takes longer to travel; how a bird sustains itself up in the air and so much more.

Da Vinci wandered the streets of Florence and often bought caged birds from the Italian merchants, opened the cages and watched the birds fly into the sky so he could understand these creatures.

He studied and drew flowers and plants from multiple angles to better understand their anatomy. According to scholar Michael Gelb, da Vinci wrote in a journal,

 Do you not see how many and how varied are the actions which are performed by men alone? Do you not see how many different kinds of animals there are, and also of trees and plants and flowers? What variety of hilly and level places, of springs, rivers, cities, public and private buildings; of instruments fitted for man's use; of diverse costumes, ornaments and arts?"

Da Vinci didn't confine his intense curiosity to botany and nature either. He interrogated his paintings by placing them against a mirror so he could better judge their strengths and weaknesses.

He even dissected human bodies to understand how our bags of flesh and bones work. He wrote about his intense curiosity.

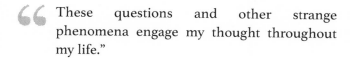 These questions and other strange phenomena engage my thought throughout my life."

Da Vinci's approach is exhausting, and I'm not advocating dissecting human bodies. However, you can develop a da Vincian kind of intense curiosity, interrogate your big ideas and figure out which to act on and which to discard by asking a simple question repeatedly: Why?

The Five Whys

Taiichi Ohno (1912-1990) had a mission. As a production engineer, he wanted to eliminate waste and inefficiency in the production processes he was responsible for at Toyota.

As a shop floor supervisor, Ohno knew firsthand how many components Toyota stockpiled for its production line at great expense. When he became an executive, he adopted a da Vincian approach to this problem and asked senior management why the company adhered to such a costly solution.

Not satisfied with their answers, Ohno kept asking "*Why?*" until he got to the root of why the company believed it needed its stockpiles.

Ohno also questioned why Toyota needed to buy specialised, expensive and difficult to customise machines when general purpose, smaller machines were cheaper, could produce a wider variety of parts and be reconfigured.

He developed his method of interrogative questioning

into a problem-solving tool known as the Five Whys. He then set out instructing engineers at Toyota how they could use the Five Whys to fix and prevent issues every day on the manufacturing line.

When confronted with a problem, have you ever stopped and asked why five times? It's hard to do even though it sounds easy. Ohno used the example of a machine that stopped functioning:

1. **Why did the machine stop?** There was an overload and the fuse blew.
2. **Why was there an overload?** The bearing was not sufficiently lubricated.
3. **Why was it not lubricated sufficiently?** The lubrication pump was not pumping sufficiently.
4. **Why was it not pumping sufficiently?** The shaft of the pump was worn and rattling.
5. **Why was the shaft worn out?** There was no strainer attached, and metal scrap got in.

The Five Whys became a problem-solving tool at Toyota and other manufacturing companies. In the *Lean Startup*, Eric Reis explained,

> The Toyota production system has been rebuilt on the practise and evolution of this scientific approach. By asking and answering "why" five times we can get to the real reason for the problem, which is often hidden behind more obvious symptoms."

Asking "why" five times like this can help uncover most problems and address the underlying causes.

In the same way, you can solve creative problems and figure out what to do next by applying it to your work.

Several years ago, I kept a blog called WorkReadPlay. Over the course of a year, I published posts about productivity, technology, games and other ramblings.

As my website traffic grew, I discovered many visitors left after they landed on my site. I couldn't figure out how to convince people to read my work.

I knew I needed help, so I joined a blogging training programme, and I asked a mentor to review my website. He told me the name of my site was confusing visitors.

The term "WorkReadPlay" didn't communicate what my blog was about, and my website visitors had little patience for figuring it out for themselves. I wasn't happy with his analysis because changing a site name is a lot of work. So, I used the Five Whys to figure out what to do next.

1. **Why do I want to rename my blog?** The current name is confusing for new visitors, and they leave almost immediately.
2. **Why is this name confusing?** The terms Work, Read, and Play don't relate to the articles I write about, and I often find myself having to explain to people what the blog title or name means.
3. **Why doesn't this name relate to the articles I write?** I'm more interested in publishing articles about writing and creativity than in posting articles about work, books, games or life in general.
4. **Why am I more interested in writing these kinds of articles?** I feel more confident writing these kinds of articles because it's what I'm

passionate about. This sort of writing will enable
me to become a better writer and even help
people.

5. **Why do I want to become a better writer and
    help people?** So I can earn a living from my
    writing and find more meaning from my work.

It took me ten minutes to ask the Five Whys. In the same
way, this creative problem-solving tool will help you overcome creative challenges and identify the cause of what's
holding you back.

Now that you understand how to ask better questions
about your big idea, you'll need a place to record your
answer.

The Creative Power of Journal Writing

Whether you like to write or not, journalling is an ideal
practise for thinking through a big idea. It will help you
identify negative thought patterns, set goals and track your
progress. It will also help you articulate arguments and
ideas privately.

You can also reflect on recent lessons from your
personal or professional life and mark accomplishments
and failures.

I've kept journals in various forms for ten years. It's
entertaining and sometimes worrying to read back on
personal and professional journal entries from several
years ago.

A journal isn't about impressing others with your ability
to craft a great sentence. Instead, it serves as a place for you

to ask better questions and record your answers. These could include:

- What do I know about my big idea?
- What do I need to find out about my big idea?
- What's wrong with my big idea?
- What's inspired about my big idea?
- Why do I want to create this?
- Why do I feel blocked?
- Why does this inspire me?
- How can I approach my big idea in an original way?
- What will happen if my big idea fails?
- What will happen if my big idea succeeds?

Some people want to keep a journal but say they find the process time consuming, that they forget to write regular entries and that they don't know what to write.

If you're experiencing these problems, accept that there will be times when you don't or can't write. You don't have to write long or literary entries. Sometimes 100 or even 200 words will be enough to consider your idea in a new way.

Yes, journal writing demands commitment, consistency and honesty, but the creative process will impose these on you anyway.

Start Asking Better Questions Today

I was a care worker in the community for two difficult years.

Finally, after a spending a weekend ticking charts, cleaning toasters, dusting behind the presses, administering medication, teaching the residents how to shop and cook for themselves, checking the household car for defects and writing lengthy reports about everything I did or didn't do, I came home and argued with my wife.

"I can't deal with the depth of madness in that place, and my manager is complaining about my inability to clean the place," I said. "They want us to be caretakers, cleaners, doctors, nurses, mechanics personal assistants and more, and it's never enough. Why do I have to put up with their unrealistic expectations?"

"You don't," my wife said.

"What do you mean?"

"If you hate the job so much, why don't you just quit?"

"That's a ridiculous idea," I said. "I need a paying job. Why would you say something like that? You don't understand what I've to put up with."

"I understand more than you realise."

I went upstairs to write about our argument, but instead I reread old entries from my journal. I paused when I found this one:

 After I had come home from work last Thursday, I sat in the car outside the house for 20 minutes in silence. When I managed to go inside, I could barely speak to my wife. It was all I could do to go straight to bed.

Last night I had a review. [My manager] said she wished I was less argumentative. She told me I need to make more of an effort with the house cleaning.

She has a point, but what galls me is being criticised for not cleaning the crumbs out of a toaster. Crumbs in a fucking toaster? Maybe we should all live in cellophane wraps and never leave our disinfected and whitewashed beds?

This morning, HR told me they're not calling me for an interview for a promotion because the director of nursing doesn't recognise my qualification.

Is this the shove out the door I need rather than the hand on the shoulder that says, "Stay a while longer?" Why am I wasting my time in a job I hate?"

If I knew about the Five Whys several years ago, I would have quit my job immediately, but even being forced to answer one 'Why' was enough for me to reconsider my wife's suggestion.

Over the course of a few weeks, I realised I was working somewhere that didn't value creativity or curiosity from its employees.

I handed in my notice.

It took another two years (and a stint of unemployment) before I found satisfying work, but I wouldn't change how things worked out.

Asking why got me into trouble, but it also helped me figure out I was the wrong person in the wrong job.

Curiosity can be a dangerous thing.

Most people don't like asking difficult questions because they're afraid of the answers. They might have to quit a job they hate, abandon a big idea they love or pivot the direction of their creative project in a more challenging direction.

You and I know better.

We anticipate unexpected problems. We recognise them as signs we're asking the right questions. We understand that cultivating intense curiosity is the best way to figure where we're going with our big idea and what we should create next.

Creative Takeaways

- Got a creative problem? Ask 'Why' five times until you get to the root of it.
- Start a journal about your creative project and record your progress each day. Write like no one will read it.

BE OPEN, BE PURPOSEFUL

"While you're being creative, nothing is wrong, there is no such thing as a mistake – any dribble may lead to the breakthrough."
– John Cleese

We take this substance for granted today, but in the 1830s, the western world was in the grip of rubber fever. A series of inventors were determined to earn money from selling waterproof fabrics, clothing, tubes and storage implements all made from rubber.

They faced a number of problems.

Natural rubber is messy and inelastic. It freezes solid during cold winters and turns into a glue-like substance during hot summers.

Within five years, many of the companies selling natural rubber goods went bankrupt, and people agreed natural rubber had no future.

A self-taught chemist from Connecticut by the name of Charles Goodyear (1800–1860) took exception to common wisdom about rubber. Goodyear dedicated his life to his one big idea: That he could treat natural rubber and transform it into a usable substance for mass-market customers.

"There is probably no other inert substance which so excites the mind," he said about rubber.

Goodyear experimented unsuccessfully with the material for years throughout great personal hardship and often on the verge of bankruptcy.

Six of his twelve children died in infancy, and he was imprisoned for being unable to pay his bills. His regular exposure to dangerous chemicals like nitric acid, which he used to treat rubber, harmed his health, and he even almost accidentally suffocated himself.

Goodyear hit a turning point in 1839. He went into the Woburn General Hardware Store in Massachusetts to sell a sample of natural rubber combined with sulphur and white lead to prospective buyers.

While showing his product to a sceptical audience, Goodyear accidentally threw a fistful of gum onto a hot potbellied stove. It sizzled and turned hard under the heat, and when Goodyear scraped the substance off the stove, he found the rubber charred like leather.

Most men would have seen this as an embarrassing disaster but not Goodyear. He realised that heat held the key to treating natural rubber.

An almost bankrupt Goodyear spent the following winter figuring out how much heat he had to apply to natural rubber and for how long to achieve this effect.

Eventually, he discovered that applying steam to rubber under pressure for four to six hours provided the intended results.

Goodyear denied his discovery of vulcanization was a mere happy accident.

Instead, he insisted the hot stove incident held meaning only for someone "whose mind was prepared to draw an inference," for someone who had "applied himself most perseveringly to the subject."

If you want your mind to draw an inference between different ideas, like Goodyear, you must open yourself up to what's possible. And if you want to apply yourself perseveringly to your subject, be purposeful about how you act on your big ideas.

Open Yourself Up

Goodyear probably didn't feel at ease pitching his wares in a hardware store full of sceptics, and there's no need to put yourself through this additional torment; it's hard enough to unlock fresh thinking.

To open yourself up to better ideas like Goodyear did, you'll need time, space and freedom to think, which is why the early mornings or late nights are ideal for creative projects.

Once you're there, relax your focus. It helps to read a book or listen to music you love before you start and then to prepare your workspace for making a mess.

You should feel more relaxed, playful and even humorous about your work and about making mistakes.

Cultivate an environment without consequences, bad ideas or expectations to perform. For 30 or 60 minutes let it be enough to have fun with your crazy ideas, to embrace the chaos. Enjoy curiosity for its own sake and see where it takes you.

When you do, absurd ideas will float to the top of your mind, and you'll find it easier to grab them and draw elaborate connections between different concepts.

Having fun is an essential element. If something doesn't feel like work, you're more likely to enjoy what you're doing or at least think differently about the challenges you're facing. If a creative project feels like work, inspired thinking is less likely.

Opening yourself up means experimenting, playing with the ridiculous and with statements or questions like:

- What would happen if...?
- Wouldn't it be even better if...?
- Let's pretend
- Go on

John Cleese (b. 1939) is a British actor and comedy writer famous for films like *A Fish Called Wanda* and the *Monty Python* series, as well as television shows like *Fawlty Towers*. An expert on creativity, he describes opening your mind up to new ideas as being in the open mode.

He said,

> The open mode is a relaxed, expansive, less purposeful mode in which we are probably more contemplative, more inclined to humour ... and consequently more playful."

Cleese, like many creative masters, plays with his problems when he wants to open himself up to new ways of thinking. He avoids coming to a decision about what needs to be done and finds time for exploration and happy accidents by creating as free an atmosphere as possible for himself and those he works with.

 It's a mode in which curiosity for its own sake

can operate because we're not under pressure to get a specific thing done quickly. We can play and that is what allows our natural creativity to surface."

Like Cleese, try new forms of creative expression that you haven't mastered and see where they go. To find new ideas that matter, allow yourself to commit mistakes and only later decide which of these you want to fix and which belong in the bin.

At first, you might not have a clue as to what a great idea looks like or what you'll do when one arrives. Although Cleese likens being open to having fun, it also takes guts to do something new.

Zoom into a single detail in your work (as Goodyear did with his sizzled piece of rubber), play around with your arrangements and see if your ideas unravel or tighten up.

Then zoom out, take the wider view and explore what would happen if you changed the medium, form or direction of your idea.

Once you've unlocked new ideas or found a way of thinking differently about your work, it's time to put what you've come up with into action.

Be Purposeful

If being open helps you become a more creative artist, being purposeful will help you become a more productive artist.

To be purposeful is to adopt an active state of mind wherein you focus entirely on the task at hand.

Being purposeful is what you do when you're under deadline, when you face multiple demands or when you're at work.

This mindset feels exciting and sometimes anxious. There's pressure to achieve a goal within a certain time-frame, and that pressure spurs you into concentrated action.

It's what Goodyear did after the incident in the Woburn general hardware store when he set out to determine how much heat to apply to treat natural rubber. Goodyear knew what he needed to do; he just had to figure out how to accomplish that goal.

Cleese likens being purposeful to being in the closed mode.

> We have inside...a feeling that's there's lots to be done and we have to get on with it if we're going to get through it all. It's an active, probably slightly anxious mode, although the anxiety can be exciting and pleasurable.
>
> It's a mode in which we are probably a little impatient if only with ourselves. It has a little tension in it, not much humour. It's a mode in which we are very purposeful and it's a mode in which we can get very stressed and even a little bit manic but not creative."

Be purposeful when you need to accomplish a series of set tasks under a tight deadline. To integrate this thinking into your creative work, eliminate as many distractions as possible from your studio. Turn off email, the television or even distracting background music.

Your routine and the work before you is all that matters. Don't stop to ask why or ponder your motivations. If for example, you're about to jump out of a plane, it's unhelpful to consider the myriad of absurd uses for a broken para-chute. Focus on nailing your landing.

Remember, you're on the hook for meeting a deadline, for finishing a project on time and for realising the demands of others.

Ask yourself, "What's the next action for my creative project?"

If you are creating as part of a team, ensure everyone knows what they are doing and they have what they need to finish on time.

Do everything in your power to complete this action and push your creative project towards its inevitable and final outcome.

But what should you do if the scale of your project is overwhelming?

If that's the case, then chunk or break down your creative work into smaller, more digestible pieces. Tackle each of these pieces in the most efficient way possible using your limited resources.

Let's say I want to research a scene for a short story that's set in a Spanish seafood restaurant.

First, I'll write down everything I have to research about this scene on a list. This might include finding a picture of the restaurant, figuring out the food on the menu, determining the location of the restaurant and writing down descriptions of the restaurant's employees and clientele.

Next, I allocate a 15-minute period during which I research these items and nothing else. Later on, I'll concentrate on writing the scene .

When it's time to write this scene, I avoid feeling overwhelmed about what I need to do because I have everything I need in one place, and I don't have to alternate between researching and writing.

Similarly, as a writer with a blog I sometimes write down a list of everything I need to do when I log into my website. This list might include: Uploading images, revising old posts and preparing the following week's post. I try to do these activities one after the other when I log in.

By listing these steps, I don't waste time repeatedly logging into my site to perform tasks during the week. I can spend more time writing and less time tinkering with my blog and others things that will pull my attention from my work.

Chunking your tasks will help you get more from the hours in your day and avoid wasting time wondering what you need to do and when.

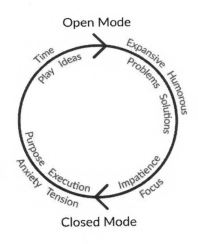

The open and closed mode

Lowering the Drawbridge

When I've a series of set tasks to perform or a To Do list to tick off, I dive in. I relish knowing what to do and when, the march towards a deadline, a completed project or published article.

Now don't get me wrong, I'm not superhuman. Like Cleese says, when I face too many demands, I feel anxious about a project failing or letting someone down.

So, I pause what I'm doing. I remember I'll get there if I have the energy, persistence and guts to complete the daily tasks forming my day.

I don't pause for long because when I'm purposeful, there's little room for self-doubt. I don't have hours to waste wrestling fears: I'm not good enough, what I'm doing will bring shame to my friends and family or I'm inventing shit as I go along.

Onward.

I'm more comfortable with being purposeful than I am with opening myself up because when I lower the draw-bridge, I invite loneliness inside.

Cleese talks about the humour of being open, but I've found it to be a darker place than he describes.

I get up early, sit at my desk and type. There, sand-wiched between the hours of 6:00 and 8:00 a.m., I look at the clock and wonder, "How much longer?" and "Can I really do this?"

I lack clarity about what I need to do. I often can't see the solution to whatever creative problem I'm working on. There's no immediate feedback about the quality of my ideas and whole days go by where I produce nothing of value. I have to remind myself production isn't the point.

I have time and space, and it'll have to be enough because turning up is a part of life.

When you're purposeful, the worst that can happen is you will let others down. When you open yourself up and lower the drawbridge, you risk inviting inside loneliness, boredom and self-doubt. Although these might be unwelcome guests, you must trust they come carrying gifts.

What do I mean by gifts?

If you look closely at your uncomfortable emotions, vulnerabilities, inner fears and desires, you'll find new ideas you can use for your creative work.

Can you use the times your parents said you weren't good enough and that you'd end up in prison one day?

Can you bring the awful sense of isolation we'll do anything to escape and turn it into a bold and original work?

Can you expose how we complain about being too busy to get anything done when we're just putting off our most important work?

Can you use the loneliness, guilt and sense of disconnect that comes with spending so much time alone with your ideas?

Can you use the time you lay in bed awake at 3:00 a.m., your daughter sick with the flu, worrying about being fired and your hair turning grey?

Can you describe the party where you drank half a bottle of absinthe, insulted the host and passed out in the bathroom?

Can you tell us about shouting at your six-year-old son to hurry up for school, him trudging behind you unhappily to the childminder and then later that day coming home from work to find he'd tidied the back garden.

He says, 'Are you happy with me now, Dad?'

And so on.

OK, I've ripped some of these examples straight from the negative thought processes that keep me up at night but don't get me wrong.

I share them here not because I want to, but to show you

that being open isn't always fun and that you must do it anyway. The world doesn't respond to homogeneous fluffy pink clouds.

Even Cleese once wrote an angry little stand-up comedy routine based on his painful and expensive second divorce.

And what did he call the tour? *Alimony*.

Great ideas speak a universal truth, at the core of which are real and often painful experiences like divorce and emotions like anger. And of course, when you open up your veins onto the blank page or the virgin canvas, there's no guarantee that anyone will like what you leave behind. That's the risk you have to take.

People will judge you, and they could even dislike you, and that's less attractive than being the kind of person who gets things done, but it's real creative work.

Your Reward

Naturally, creativity isn't a tidy process whereby you calmly walk from A to B to C and get to the end of your project without encountering problems along the way. No matter how much you prepare and plan, understand that to write, to perform, to compose is messy.

Being open to new ideas and being purposeful about how you act on them doesn't guarantee you financial or professional success, either.

Today, treated rubber is one of the most commonly used substances in the world. It's in your car, clothes and even your computer. What's more, global demand for the substance is worth $158 billion, as of 2018. Considering the value of rubber, you'd think Goodyear died a wealthy man. You'd be wrong.

Even after discovering the correct formula for the

vulcanization of rubber, Goodyear struggled personally and professionally.

British inventor Thomas Hancock patented the vulcanization process in the UK eight weeks before Goodyear, and Goodyear also had to fight a series of legal cases in the US against people who stole his ideas.

He died in 1860 some $200,000 in debt, but despite his apparent lack of success, did he die a bitter man?

No. Goodyear cared less about the outputs from his creative work and more about the effort he'd put into growing his big idea. A master of his inner genius, for Goodyear it was enough to go to the river with his bucket and draw from it over and over.

He wrote, "Life should not be estimated exclusively by the standard of dollars and cents. I am not disposed to complain that I have planted and others have gathered the fruits. A man has cause for regret only when he sows and no one reaps."

Creative Takeaways

- Spend 15 minutes playing with your creative project this week. Take a responsible, creative risk.
- If you're struggling to finish one of your ideas, break it into chunks that you tackle day by day.

UNLOCKING YOUR INNER GENIUS

"I don't paint things. I only paint the difference between things."
– Henri Matisse

Creative heroes like Matisse, Jobs and Tharp can teach us how to accomplish our dreams and overcome setbacks.

Look to their lives and works when your own is faltering and you need new ways of overcoming troubling creative impasses.

My first creative hero was English author Roald Dahl (1916-1990).

I came across him when I was five while reading books like *The BFG* and *James and the Giant Peach*.

He was the first author who showed me what's possible with the written word.

Dahl wasn't always a writer. As a young man, he worked for Shell in Kenya and Tanzania and spent his free time hunting. During World War II, Dahl became a decorated fighter ace and intelligence officer.

He shot down at least two enemy JU-88 planes, took part in the Battle Of Athens and was one of the last pilots to withdraw from Greece during the German invasion.

When he started to write, Dahl wasn't afraid to draw from the river of his old life for his new creative one. He wrote several short stories about his time as a fighter pilot and drew extensively on his previous careers in his novels and short stories.

In *James and the Giant Peach*, the seagulls (or fighter aeroplanes) attack the giant airborne peach, a talking centipede falls (or parachutes) off the giant peach, and the end of the book references air raids and heroes returning home (from the war).

Then, in *Going Solo*, Dahl wrote:

 I was already beginning to realise that the only way to conduct oneself in a situation where bombs rained down and bullets whizzed past, was to accept the dangers and all the consequences as calmly as possible. Fretting and sweating about it all was not going to help."

Dahl was a disciplined creative professional too. He came down to the river with his bucket, writing for two hours each morning and evening in a six-by-seven foot shed at the back of his orchard in Buckinghamshire, in the United Kingdom.

In his shed or "little nest," Dahl kept a comfortable chair, a lamp, a system for storing his files, a wooden desk and writing utensils.

Each day after he wrote, Dahl ate a bar of chocolate and crunched the wrappers up into a ball. He also covered the walls with pictures of his family, ideas for stories and other personal mementos.

I like this story about Dahl best of all.

Like many creative people, Dahl was having trouble finding a good idea for a project he was working on. One day while sitting behind dozens of moving cars, he suddenly thought of a breakthrough for his story.

Dahl looked around the car for a pen or a pencil to write down his idea, but he couldn't find anything and he grew afraid he'd forget his idea before getting home.

(If you ever had the unsettling experience of coming up with a great idea in the shower, while cooking, driving, walking or doing something else, you'll understand Dahl's fear.)

Dahl wasn't the kind of creative person to let a good idea flow through his hand.

So he opened his door, and with his finger wrote the word "chocolate" into the dirt on his car. This little act of plunging his bucket into the river was enough for Dahl to remember his idea, and it became *Charlie and the Chocolate Factory*.

He later said about his ideas, "You work it out and play around with it. You doodle . . . you make notes . . . it grows, it grows . . . "

Your Bucket Is Overflowing

Ideas are exciting. If you plunge your bucket deep enough into the river, you'll have more than you know what to do with.

Quench your thirst with the teachings, works and thoughts of creative masters you admire. Drink deeply from the buckets of their powerful big ideas, the crazy little ideas and even those other ideas people missed.

Ask how you can apply their approaches to your work. Intense curiosity is why creative masters like da Vinci and Jobs were successful in multiple fields like art, engineering and business. They took what worked in one field and applied it to the next.

I talk about Jobs, Tharp and Dahl, but there's just one problem with heroes. Their achievements are so lofty that it can hurt to wander through Dream Country for too long.

When this happens to you, put down your hero's work and look to your environment. A walk through a field, a farmer cutting hay, a snippet of music, a snapshot from your dream could spark fresh thinking if you let it.

Start creating something of your own, make messy mistakes, move past them and keep at your craft.

Practise opening your mind to the wider world because to be an outsider is to possess a perspective creative masters crave.

From the moment you held a guitar, a pen or a paint-brush in your hands, you might have known what kind of creative person you are, but if you haven't had this startling experience, don't worry.

Taking little risks and experimenting with form and substance will teach you more about a craft than any moment of inspiration, introspection or deep study ever can.

So keep turning up in front of the blank page or canvas.

Don't feel like any of this is a waste of time. Setbacks and dead-ends are par for the course.

Eventually, something will pop out onto the page, the screen or your sketchpad and you'll wonder, "Where did that come from?"

As you develop your creative practise, you'll be able to transfer your skills from one project or medium to the next and solve problems faster. You'll know what to borrow, what to use and what to pour back into the river.

You are your own golden ticket.

THE POWER OF CREATIVITY (BOOK 3)

HOW TO CONQUER PROCRASTINATION, FINISH YOUR WORK AND FIND SUCCESS

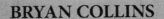

BRYAN COLLINS

THE POWER OF
CREATIVITY

HOW TO CONQUER PROCRASTINATION,
FINISH YOUR WORK AND
FIND SUCCESS (BOOK 3)

1

THE BOND

"I pay no attention whatever to anybody's praise or blame. I simply follow my own feelings."
– Wolfgang Amadeus Mozart

It seems impossible . . .

Austrian composer Wolfgang Amadeus Mozart wrote his first symphony when he was eight years of age. American writer Stephen King has published more than 55 novels and 200 short stories.

Painter Pablo Picasso created over 50,000 artworks, including 1,885 paintings during his lifetime.

American choreographer Twyla Tharp has produced or choreographed more than 100 ballet and dance shows for the theatre and for multiple films and TV shows, and she has written three popular books.

Their accomplishments are bold, their ideas big and powerful and their creative habits prolific.

Do these creative masters possess an abundance of

talent the rest of us can only dream of? Or have they found a lost, powerful secret about becoming more creative or productive?

These questions troubled me.

So I set out to understand how creative masters like Mozart and Tharp finish so many creative projects with so much success. I found that while talent is important – Mozart was a genius – it takes hundreds if not thousands of little ideas to create a single big idea.

If you find the prospect of finishing hundreds or thousands of small things off-putting (or exhausting), don't worry. Each little idea you complete accumulates like molecules inside a cell. They bond together until they possess a life of their own.

The best part is everyone has what it takes to finish their little ideas. You can finish a little idea today.

You just have to start.

Who This Book is For

This book is the *third in a three-part series* about creativity that I wrote for new writers, musicians, filmmakers and artists.

The first book, *The Power of Creativity: Learning How to Build Lasting Habits, Face Your Fears and Change Your Life*, was for writers, artists and musicians who felt adrift.

The second book, *The Power of Creativity: An Uncommon Guide to Mastering Your Inner Genius and Finding New Ideas That Matter,* focused on where to look for great ideas.

This third book is for anyone who has a great idea (or even just a little one), but they're finding it difficult to act on it, go deep into their work and finish their most important creative projects.

Over the proceeding chapters, you'll discover how to unlock a mindset for finishing your ideas, shipping your work and moving on to the next thing.

As in the previous books, I'll pull studies from academia and the business world and mix these findings with contemporary and personal examples so you can get your ideas over the finish line.

At the end of each chapter I include "Creative Takeaways" you can use to nudge your work towards its inevitable conclusion.

A Finished Creative Work

In a sentence: How to take a great idea and act on it.

But let's go deeper.

Extroverts thrive when working in the company of others, while introverts do their best work alone. So it's no surprise that many accomplished creative masters are introverts who go to great pains to work in a solitary environment.

Now it takes a degree of focus and, yes, even obsession to sit by yourself in a room in front of the blank page, canvas or a computer screen and work on an idea for hours, days, weeks and months.

Sometimes, it takes extreme measures to get your ideas over the line.

Does this sound alarming?

Well, know obsession is something you can embrace rather than fear with the right approach.

You can conquer your fear by testing your ideas, showing drafts of your book, album or art to an inner circle and getting constructive critical feedback. Or sell early versions of your ideas to beta or first customers and use their feedback to improve your craft.

As you draw towards the end of a creative project, it's natural to spend time polishing your idea into something that shines, and this is where many people get stuck.

They spend ages working on an almost-ready idea without shipping anything. They get stuck on one little idea when they should let what they have bond together and then move onto the next one.

I'll reveal the different kinds of perfectionism you must watch out for and give you practical strategies for overcoming each one so you can finally get your work out there.

Things might get a little unpleasant before you find success. So I'm going to talk about failure and mistakes (mine mostly).

They're a critical part of deep creative work. If you find these little dark moments off-putting, understand that learning from your failures and mistakes will help you improve the quality of your finished ideas dramatically.

Besides, whatever kind of success or failure greets you at the end of a creative project is about your work and not about you.

Now, there's one thing creative people with a good idea never have enough of – and that's time.

Let's begin.

2

IMMERSE YOURSELF IN YOUR CREATIVE WORK

"You're using force. You're using your hands. You're creating. You're making that white dance."
– Ronnie O'Sullivan

"There must be some mistake," I said.

My Irish teacher took the exam paper from my hands, flicked quickly through the pages, frowned and gave it back to me.

"There's no mistake," she said tapping the large F on the front page. "You've failed your end-of-the-year Irish grammar exam."

"But I worked hard at this…"

"I don't have time to argue about it, and you have another class to go to," she said. "Take your books and get out."

In Ireland, we sit exams like these because even though Irish or Gaeilge (or Gaelic) is our native language, the majority of the country speaks English.

The Irish mostly speak Gaeilge in rural parts of Ireland known as the Gaeltacht and to prevent the death of our native tongue, secondary school students (the Irish equivalent of high-school students) study Irish.

The class was awful. Everything about the system, my classmates and even my teacher bored me. She was more interested in clipping her red nails and getting us to recite Irish grammar rules than inspiring a love of the language in her charge.

Looking back to 1998, I can't blame my Irish teacher. There's no worse place to learn or teach a language than being forced to do so for an hour a day in a sweaty classroom. As a pale and spotty fourteen-year-old, I lacked the motivation and the curiosity required to excel anyway.

After school, I went home and told my parents I'd failed one of my summer exams.

They decided to help me get around this problem (or perhaps shove me through it) by sending me on a three-week holiday to a Gaeltacht summer school in Galway in the West of Ireland.

On the first night in the Gaeltacht, the head of the school or the *príomhoíde*, a tall man with a red face and sweeping black hair, marched up and down the hall holding a hurley (a wooden stick used to play hurling).

"You're Irish, and you're from Ireland!" he told 300 shell-shocked teenagers. "While you're here in the Gaeltacht, you will eat, breathe and sleep Irish. You'll dream in Irish by the time you go home."

The príomhoíde raised his hurley as though it were a talisman and he was a shaman about to bestow great knowledge upon us.

"Now tell me why must you speak Irish?"

"Because . . . " a few students replied.

"Because we're Irish," he said.

"Because we're Irish," said the students.

"Louder!"

"BECAUSE WE'RE IRISH!"

At first, doing nothing but speaking Irish struck me as a terrible way to spend my summer holidays, but as I looked around the hall, I saw I wasn't the only pale and spotty teenager who'd been sent to the Gaeltacht by his parents.

The 300 of us were in this together. It was three weeks away from our parents and, even more importantly, three weeks in the (supervised) company of the opposite sex.

Each morning, we attended an informal class in a local school where we wrote and read Gaeilge. Thankfully, there were no painful grammar exams or a teacher more interested in her red nails than us.

In the afternoon, we played traditional Irish sports like hurling and football, and we went to the beach to swim, windsurf and canoe in the sea. At night, we went to Irish dances or ceilí where they played Irish music.

Think of it as a Hogwarts for Irish kids.

I had a lot of firsts in the Gaeltacht.

I won't lie. I found the first day or two of speaking solely in Irish difficult. Like most of the students, I felt awkward and embarrassed about my inability to talk to the opposite sex *and* in our native tongue, but because everyone around me spoke Irish from breakfast to supper, this awkwardness passed.

I was excited about being away from home for so long for the first time. Better still, I knew what was expected of me: Avoid speaking in English at all costs or risk the wrath of the príomhóide and his hurley. Unlike when I was in school at home, I wasn't bored.

After a week of being immersed in Irish, speaking the

language felt effortless. By the end of the three weeks I even dreamt "as Gaeilge" and most importantly, I was able to successfully chat up a girl in Irish.

If you want to become more creative, immersing yourself in your work, at least for a time, will help you bond your ideas and accomplish more with them.

Making the White Dance

Ronnie O'Sullivan (b. 1975) performs his creative work in warm halls decorated with thick carpet and low lighting. His uniform is a white or black shirt, a matching dinner jacket and trousers, and a bow tie.

His creative tools are a set of ash and ebony snooker cues and a piece of chalk, and he uses them to tame the white ball and pot the six coloured and fifteen red balls in the correct order. While he creates, a well-dressed audience watches, talking in whispers.

When O'Sullivan is at work at the table, he immerses himself in his craft. He takes command of what's happening in front of him. He feeds off his shots, creates impossible positions for his opponent, and when a game is going well, he is unstoppable.

According to a wonderful *New Yorker* profile, observers of the sport regard O'Sullivan as one of the most talented players ever. He has won 27 ranking snooker titles, including five World Championship, five Masters and five UK Championship titles.

Like many creative masters, O'Sullivan has meditated on the nature of his chosen medium. He believes if he first strikes the white cue ball the right way and it responds to his touch, he won't lose.

He says about his connection with the white ball that

he's using his hands to create, working to make "that white dance."

Phil Yates, a former snooker correspondent for British newspaper *The Times*, once compared O'Sullivan to a sage who instinctively understands mathematical equations. He argued O'Sullivan uses his insight to tame the balls before him and conquer opponents.

After a game, O'Sullivan emerges from his craft and is barely able to remember how he played or if he struck a particular coloured ball in a certain way. When sports journalists question Ronnie about an exceptional performance, he often struggles to explain what happened or how he did it.

Damien Hirst, an artist and friend of O'Sullivan, told Sam Knight of the *New Yorker,*

> I go, 'What about that pink you potted?' And he'll go, 'What pink?' He's blank. He's totally startled. It's like Van Gogh. I go, 'You did brilliantly there.' And he goes, 'Did I?'"

O'Sullivan is a master of total immersion.

Total Immersion: What You Need to Know

When you first sit down to do your work, your monkey mind darts from one task to the next, and you resist getting started. After five or 10 minutes, you wade in deeper, leaving self-doubt on the shore as your mind swims towards an idea.

You feel relaxed, comfortable and energetic about your work and for a while, all sense of time falls way.

Eventually, outside life intrudes. Your boss wants a report, the phone rings, it's time to go to work or a meeting. So you put down your pen, instrument or brush. You surface, glance at the clock, breathe in and wonder, "Where did the time go?"

Later, you look at the music you've composed, the painting you worked on, or the pages you filled and wonder, "How the hell did I do that?"

Creative masters like O'Sullivan regularly experience a state of concentration so intense that time and the wider world fade away.

Call it being in the zone, a creative fugue or a bubble as Tharp does (see book two). Call it making the white dance or a state of flow like the Hungarian psychologist Mihaly Csikszentmihalyi.

He wrote,

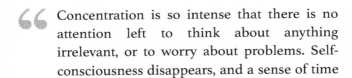 Concentration is so intense that there is no attention left to think about anything irrelevant, or to worry about problems. Self-consciousness disappears, and a sense of time becomes distorted."

When you are immersed, to play, to write, to draw, to paint, to compose...to finish feels effortless. So how can you achieve this state more often?

Pursue a Realistic Creative Challenge

First, your project must present a creative challenge and give your brain a rigorous workout, but it mustn't be so difficult that you don't know how to start.

If you're a new musician, and you want to play a guitar song, you'll find it impossible to immerse yourself if you attempt to compose a symphony. Unless you're Mozart, this creative task is too difficult.

Similarly, if you're doing something you've done a 1,000 times before, like covering The Beatles' "Yesterday", you won't face a real challenge. Instead, your mind will go on autopilot, wander and consider many other things that have nothing to do with the creative task at hand.

Be smart about it: Set the right kinds of creative goals.

A **good goal** is one you can achieve if you push yourself. A **better goal** takes a serious amount of work and resources to complete, and the **best goal** is an ideal scenario or a "reach for the stars" endeavour.

Here's an example for writers:

- **Good goal:** I will write a 60,000-word contemporary fiction novel this year.
- **Better goal:** I will write and sell 2,000 copies of a 60,000-word contemporary fiction novel in the next 12 months.
- **Best goal:** I will write a best-selling 60,000-word novel and hit the *New York Times* best-seller list within the next two years.

Each of these goals is challenging in its way and requires increasing amounts of mental focus and resources to move from one to the next.

Goal one is achievable unless you spend your days watching television. The second goal requires you to learn marketing skills and get outside of your comfort zone. The third goal is unattainable without the guidance of a mentor, marketing professional or a best-selling author.

If you set good/better/best goals, you'll gain more opportunities to push yourself and your creative projects forward and succeed at different levels.

You can always acquire the resources and skills as you go, and if while creating you realise the goals are missing the mark, you can modify them.

Devour Other People's Big Ideas

What athletes put into their bodies reflects what they put out on the track or in the swimming pool. When you're working on your ideas, remember that what you put into your mind reflects what comes out in your work.

As part of a 2012 scientific study, published in the *Scientific Study of Literature*, researchers gave participants one of eight stories or essays to read.

These stories included Frank O'Connor's "My Oedipus Complex" and Jean Stafford's "Night Club". The essays included Rabindranath Tagore's "East and West" and Henri Bergson's "Why Do We Laugh?"

Before they started reading these stories, each participant took a standard test of the so-called big five personality traits: extroversion, neuroticism, openness, agreeableness and conscientiousness.

The participants also rated how they were feeling on a scale of zero to 10 for ten different emotions. After reading the assigned text, the participants were again given a personality test and asked to rate their emotions.

Participants who read an artistic story or essay changed their personality scores more than those who judged what they'd read to be less artistic. In other words, they were transformed by other people's big ideas.

The implications are clear. It's not enough though to dine out on other people's ideas like a passive consumer.

You must extract lessons from these ideas, reflect on why they matter, and then let these ideas transform you from the inside out.

If you're a writer, read often and outside of your comfort zone. If you're a musician, expose yourself to new and beautiful types of music and even to songs you hate so you'll know what your system resists.

If you're an artist, visit inspiring exhibitions and tear apart the works and thought processes of Henri Matisse, Pablo Picasso and other creative masters.

Disconnect

Digital tools simplify the act of creation and enable you to remix, edit and share your big ideas with others in a way that wasn't possible for Amadeus Mozart or Albert Einstein.

They're also confining.

In a 2014 paper published in the *Psychological Science* journal US researchers, Pam Mueller and Daniel Oppenheimer found note-taking with a pen instead of a laptop gives students a better understanding of the subject in question. In other words, digital cuts quickly, but the pen cuts deeply.

When I'm writing and struggling with an idea, I sometimes want to press my hand through the screen, reach in and pull out the molecules of what I'm chasing – but this isn't possible with electronic devices.

Traditional creative tools like the brush, a guitar pick or even the snooker cue, come with fewer preconceptions than a computer and fewer distractions than the Internet.

If you're at the start of the creative process, and you're having trouble understanding your subject, go back to the basics: Shun your digital tools.

Use non-digital tools to release ideas from your head and put them somewhere you can easily rearrange them, as O'Sullivan does with the white and red balls of the snooker table.

You could mind map your ideas on a whiteboard, write down what you know about your topic on paper or even use index cards to order the themes of work.

Later on, when you've got the genesis of an idea, transfer it to your digital tool and execute on it.

Refuse Side Attractions

Use the word "No" to leave time consuming side attractions on the shore and wade into your creative work. This isn't rude or impolite; creative masters say no all the time.

Charles Dickens (1812-1870) wrote more than a dozen novels and numerous short stories and essays. He did it by saying no and by focusing on his big ideas. He said,

> 'It is only half an hour' - 'It is only an afternoon' - 'It is only an evening,' people say to me over and over again; but they don't know that it is impossible to command one's self sometimes to any stipulated and set disposal of five minutes – or that the mere consciousness of an engagement will sometime worry a whole day."

Dickens is in fine company. Canadian-American writer and Pulitzer Prize winner Saul Bellow (b. 1915) cultivated a habit of saying no. His secretary explained,

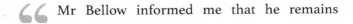 Mr Bellow informed me that he remains

creative in the second half of life, at least in
part, because he does not allow himself to be a
part of other people's 'studies.'"

Be firm but polite when you refuse someone. If you feel
under pressure to say yes, explain you're working on a
creative project, you're close to a deadline and that you'll
return to their request as soon as you're free. Then, make a
point to do so.

When someone in authority makes a request, like a
manager asking for a report, don't attend to it immediately
unless it's urgent. Write this request down on your To-Do
list and get back to work. Then, when you've finished,
review your list and evaluate which requests you need to
act upon.

This way you can refuse the interruption while giving
the appearance of having said yes to the person.

Setting clear boundaries at home helps too. Let your
spouse, your family or your friends know you've put time
aside to work on your ideas at morning or at night.

At first, they might have questions or requests while
you're working, but eventually, those closest to you will
come to understand (or at least respect) your boundaries.

Remember to Come up for Air

When you immerse yourself in what you're doing, you're
able to organise your consciousness, ideas and inner
resources without overthinking it. You become more respon-
sive to your inner feelings, what you like and dislike, and a
more honest version of your big ideas will emerge.

Sounds great, right?

Caution: The annals of creativity are full of stories about

writers who became recluses like J.D. Salinger and artists like Picasso, who lost themselves in their work and resented the intrusion of the outside world.

Immersion is an addictive state that feels more comfortable than engaging with the wider world.

Csikszentmihalyi wrote,

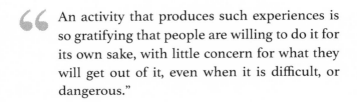

> An activity that produces such experiences is so gratifying that people are willing to do it for its own sake, with little concern for what they will get out of it, even when it is difficult, or dangerous."

He also cites American chess master Bobby Fischer (1943-2008) as an example of a creative master who lost his way. In 1958, aged just 15, Fischer became the youngest grandmaster of his generation. He dominated his contemporaries for much of his career.

Chess is a game that demands intense mental concentration for hours at a time, but outside of the game Fischer was an inept, unhappy and even unpleasant person. After his chess career ended, he wandered from Hungary, Germany, Philippines, Japan and later to Iceland.

In 2001, he made a series of anti-American and anti-Semitic remarks, and Fischer even told a reporter he hoped there would be a military coup d'état in his home country.

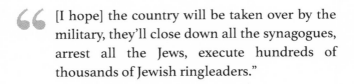

> [I hope] the country will be taken over by the military, they'll close down all the synagogues, arrest all the Jews, execute hundreds of thousands of Jewish ringleaders."

The U.S. Chess Federation evicted Fischer from the

organisation. Subsequently, Fischer campaigned for his US citizenship to be revoked. He spent the remainder of his life in Iceland until he died in 2008.

You must understand that the experience of total immersion, though gratifying, won't make you any happier in day-to-day life.

O'Sullivan has had a chaotic life outside of sport. In 1991, his father "Big Ron" was imprisoned for 18 years because he killed another man in a nightclub fight, and today their relationship is strained.

He also faces struggles that have nothing to do with snooker, something many of us can empathise with. He has three children, but his relationships with their mothers broke down.

O'Sullivan has fought alcohol and drugs, and he once told a reporter he tried all the different Anonymous groups (including Narcotics Anonymous and Sex Anonymous) out of a sense of incompleteness. He's sought help from several different psychiatrists and gurus and has explored Christianity, Buddhism and Islam.

Creative immersion will propel your work, but it can't fulfil you entirely.

All It Takes

My summer Gaeltacht romance didn't survive more than a couple of weeks, but my newfound confidence with the Irish language lasted longer.

Can you guess what happened when I went back to secondary school in September?

I was able to understand our Irish textbooks and, even more surprisingly, what our teacher was saying during our complex grammar classes.

After spending my summer holidays totally immersed in Irish, I was primed and ready for anything an uninterested teacher and simple grammar exam could throw at me.

You don't need to be a creative master like Einstein or O'Sullivan to immerse yourself in your craft.

Set yourself realistic challenges, devour other people's ideas and avoid meaningless distractions. Become skilled at saying no to others because you must put your work first, if only for an hour or two each day.

Finally, unless you care little for your lasting happiness or those around you, come up for air from time to time.

We'll be waiting on the shore for you.

Creative Takeaways

- Set good/better/best goals so you can immerse yourself in your work.
- Don't stay immersed for so long that you forget yourself entirely. Remember to come up for air.

3

SEEK OUT SOLITUDE

"I live in that solitude which is painful in youth, but delicious in the years of maturity."
– Albert Einstein

You're sitting alone in a small, air-conditioned room in front of a wooden table. There's a large red button on the table, from which runs a wire to the floor and towards your leg. It's connected to a white electrode, which is pinned to your bare ankle.

Before leaving you alone in this room, a scientist said if you waited for just 15 minutes without pressing the red button you'd receive five dollars. He also said pressing the red button will administer a mild electric shock.

"Why would anyone electrocute themselves?" you asked. "I'll take the five dollars. This is the easiest money I've ever earned."

That was then, and this is now; you can't bear it any longer. There's no clock; you don't have your phone, and you've nothing to do but wrestle with your thoughts. You are alone and bored.

Your hand hovers over the button.

I wonder how strong the shock is?

A mild electric shock jolts up your leg.

Crazy right?

In 2014, neuroscientists in the United States revealed the results of a series of experiments with more than 700 people. They asked participants to spend time alone in a room for between six and 15 minutes without access to a cell phone or a writing instrument.

The participants had the option of entertaining themselves while alone by pressing a button and receiving a mild electric shock.

The neuroscientists found 64 percent of men and 15 percent of women began self-administering electric shocks when left alone to think. These same people had previously told researchers that they would pay money to avoid receiving these jolts.

Timothy Wilson and the other researchers concluded while some people are absorbed by interesting ideas and exciting fantasies, many of us lack the training and self-discipline that being alone with our thoughts requires.

 Without such training, people prefer doing to thinking, even if what they are doing is so unpleasant that they would normally pay to avoid it. The untutored mind does not like to be alone with itself."

Writing, painting, composing, story-telling and creating demand self-discipline. Although you're unlikely to face the prospects of electrocution, and you almost always will have access to your tools, these creative pursuits require intense and sustained concentration and all of the resources the left-side of your brain can muster.

To turn an idea into something worthwhile, to let it acquire a life of its own, you must find a place where you can work alone and uninterrupted for sustained periods.

Creative masters like Einstein did their best work in solitude and even today artists depend on time alone for improving their craft.

The Problems with Creating in Company

Artistic creativity is an internal act. It's also a solitary one, at least when you begin. I've nothing against collaboration and working with others – some creative projects demand it. In a celebrated and recently published essay on creativity, Isaac Asimov wrote,

 One person may know A and not B, another may know B and not A, and either knowing A and B, both may get the idea – though not necessarily at once or even soon."

You can bond your ideas with another person's. You can connect your A with their B and come up with C, provided you've shaped your idea and separated yourself from them.

If you haven't even got an idea that you're somewhat happy with, your idea will never form a life of its own. The truth is creative masters practise their craft and work on their ideas alone, at least at first.

To express yourself, examine your motivations, values, experiences and perceptions and then mine what you find for your creative work.

When you're alone, you can investigate your thoughts (or administer electric shocks), reflect on your experiences and even face your demons.

You can use time alone to isolate yourself and your ideas from overwhelming influences, and you can use this quietness to think deeply about your big idea.

When you're alone and free from distraction, you have no more excuses for procrastinating.

When you're working on a big idea with others, it's almost impossible to look deeply inside yourself. You'll worry what people think of you and fear you're being judged.

It's exceptionally difficult to avoid their influences for better or worse, and if your idea feels unreasonable, misguided or unbalanced, the company of others will muzzle the bark of your imagination.

You can't know yourself if you're concerned what others think about you or how they're going to react to your deepest thoughts.

If your collaborators are more dominant, vocal or articulate than you, their voices will drown out yours. For every one good idea you come up with, there will be a 1,000 or even 10,000 more that are embarrassing and that you won't want others to see.

When you work with a big idea in the company of others, you're more likely to be interrupted. If you're working in an office, for example, a colleague might come to you with a simple and well-meaning request.

Once you attend to this request, it takes several minutes for you to collect your thoughts after the interruption and pick up from where you left off.

In other words, this disruption delays the progress of

your idea and removes you from the warm, creative bubble you need to create.

The Science Behind Practicing Alone

Swedish psychologist K. Anders Ericsson (b. 1947) and his team examined how creative masters acquire expert knowledge in their chosen discipline. As part of an intensive study, they evaluated three kinds of violinists.

The best violinists in the study belonged to famous symphony orchestras in West Berlin such as the Berlin Philharmonic Orchestra and the Radio Symphony Orchestra.

The good violinists included students from Berlin's prestigious Hochschule der Kuenste music academy. They had the potential to develop careers as international soloists. The average violinists included those musicians training to be teachers.

All three groups practised for up to 50 hours week, and there was little difference in the amount of time each group spent playing the violin.

However, the best violinists rated working alone for an hour to an hour and a half each day as key to improving their skills. They also valued sleep as highly relevant for improving their performance, and they often napped to recover from daily practise.

As the study studied showed with the best violinists, solitude helps you identify skills you need to improve and an opportunity to work on them without interruption.

When you work alone, you have time to grow the early seeds of your idea without worrying what someone else will think or if they'll judge you. You also have the space you need to create freely.

The quiet of the early morning or late night is ideal for solitude.

Like the violinists in Ericsson's study, seek out opportunities to practise without interruption for 90 minutes. This is an ideal amount of time to practise your craft alone.

An hour and a half gives you time to pry the lid off your creative project and dive in. After swimming around in your creative juices for 90 minutes, you'll need to take a break. Any less and you'll be just getting into the flow of your creative work when the time comes to stop.

If you haven't developed a habit of creating alone, the people closest to you will question what you're doing. After all, it's worrying to see someone you know remove themselves from the wider world to work on a mysterious project.

Unless they are pursuing a creative project of their own, you may find it difficult to explain what you're trying to accomplish. I once coached a new writer who emailed me to say,

 I'm struggling with convincing my family that writing is a reasonable thing to do with my time. My friends and I have recently started a site . . . and my sister especially thinks it is stupid."

Unfortunately, these problems are normal and you will have to accept them as a cost of the creative process. It doesn't help that creating something often means rejecting one idea after the next, meaning you won't always have something tangible for your hard work and time spent in solitude.

However, as time passes and you become more accomplished at your craft, this will become an easier problem to surmount.

Einstein Did His Best Work Alone

German-born theoretical physicist Albert Einstein did his best work alone.

Before he became famous, Einstein struggled to find work in academia during his twenties. He received numerous rejection letters from would-be employers and universities where he wanted to study.

A young Einstein in need of money eventually took up work in a Swiss patent office in Bern. There, he worked as a technical expert for six days a week between 1904 and 1907.

This job was below Einstein's obvious talents and altogether apart from the rigours and confines of academia.

Einstein was often able to complete a day's work in just several hours, and he spent the remainder of the working day and his free time at night and the weekends working privately on his scientific ideas.

He wrote to a friend about his habits, "Keep in mind that besides eight hours of work, each day also has eight hours for fooling around, and then there's also Sunday."

Instead of being held back, these years were some of Einstein's most creative. While working in the Bern patent office, he released six academic papers in 1906 and another ten in 1907. He helped prove the existence of atoms, and he formulated a revolutionary quantum theory of light as well as his most famous equation: $E = mc^2$.

He moved from Germany to Switzerland and then Italy before settling in New Jersey, in the United States, working in various academic roles.

Although he roamed from country to country, Einstein

valued a quiet life that afforded him opportunities for deep thinking. He said, "the monotony of a quiet life stimulates the creative mind" and he even advocated that young scientists find jobs as lighthouse keepers so they could "devote themselves undisturbed" to thinking.

Even later on in life when Einstein achieved fame and success, he prided himself on being an outsider. He spent the latter part of his scientific career living in New Jersey searching fruitlessly for a unified theory that explained the forces of the universe.

Many of Einstein's peers and colleagues suggested he was squandering his time and creative resources on his search for a unified theory, but Einstein didn't care.

He believed he had already made his name, his position was secure and he could take risks younger colleagues couldn't afford.

What You Need to Create in Solitude

You must acquire a block of time within which to create and a willingness to guard these precious minutes against those who would take it away from you.

To acquire your block of time, determine the meaningless activities you can remove from your day, activities like watching television or consuming social media.

You could create alone late at night after you've attended to the demands of the day. The problem with this approach is you risk letting those demands sap your creative energy so that when it's time to sit down and do your work you have nothing left.

Towards the end of 2015, I attended a talk in Dublin by Dan Brown (b. 1964), author of *The Da Vinci Code*, amongst other books. The prolific author told a room of several thousand people that he gets up at 4:00 a.m. to write each day.

The presenter asked Brown if he had risen early on the morning of the talk to write.

"Yes," Brown said. "There are no emails at four in the morning. It's the most creative part of the day."

When you get up to create before the working day, you send a signal to your subconscious that your creative work comes first. Whatever else happens during the day doesn't matter because you will already have done your most important work first thing.

Next, you must guard this block of time, and to do so you're going to have to get comfortable with saying no, with passing up on opportunities and turning people down.

If you don't, others will happily fill your day with meetings, errands and tasks, that, while important to them, mean little to you. Dickens was a big believer in saying no. He said,

 Who ever is devoted to an art must be content to deliver himself wholly up to it, and to find his recompense in it. I am grieved if you suspect me of not wanting to see you, but I can't help it; I must go in my way whether or no.

It's difficult to reach for the word "no" because it has connotations of being unhelpful and even lazy.

However, every time you say "yes" to someone else's request, you are saying "no" to your creative work.

You have only a limited amount of hours each day and a finite reserve of creative energy, and you must spend this wisely. Agree to every little commitment and you risk draining all of your creative mental energy, time and resources.

Be polite but be firm, and then seek out a warm, creative bubble where nothing can intrude.

Embracing Solitude

I spend at least 90 minutes each day alone in a small room on the second floor of our house.

I've two small children, and my house is busy and loud in the evenings. I find it difficult to write for a sustained period without interruption at nighttime. Although I'm a night person, I get up most mornings two hours before work to write.

I depend on the essentials: A desk, a comfortable chair, a bookshelf, a computer, paper, pens, somewhere to put my things and a device to electrocute myself if I procrastinate!

A window in this small room looks out onto the street. I'm prone to distractions, so I minimise them by listening to instrumental music through a pair of headphones and sometimes by closing the curtains.

See? You don't need an office or a studio to create.

American short story writer and poet Raymond Carver (1938-1988) wrote many of his stories on the back of a notebook while sitting in his old car.

What's more important is that you have somewhere you can go to each day and work on your idea without interruption.

This could be the spare room in your house or apartment, a coffee shop, unused space in your workplace, a library or a quiet seat on a train. If you follow Einstein's recommendation, you can even use a lighthouse!

Like Einstein practiced, it will help you tremendously if

you can avoid wasting time by considering the practicalities of how you're going to get real creative work done each day.

Solitude, daydreams and deep introspective thinking are the hallmarks of the creative process, but many people express an intense dislike of being alone and of feeling bored.

They go to extreme lengths to avoid spending a significant amount of time in their own company with only their thoughts for entertainment.

If you want to become more creative, train yourself to enjoy spending time in your company and protect this time alone at all costs. Start small.

Cultivate a daily habit of creating in solitude for 15 or 30 minutes each day. Use this time to get more comfortable with day-dreams and the deep introspective thinking that feels like the very antithesis of doing.

Let your little ideas form, take shape, bond with each other and acquire a life of their own.

From there, slowly increase the amount of time you spend creating alone and, like a master violinist, deliberately practise your craft.

Creative Takeaways

- Find a place (a quiet room, a coffee shop, a library) where you can work on your big idea without interruption.
- Refuse or decline whatever you can get away with until you've cultivated a habit of creating for 90 minutes each day.

4
―――――

BE OBSESSED

"People do not lack strength; they lack will."
– Victor Hugo

My wife wants to know what I'm doing.

"Sitting alone in a room is a strange way to pass your time," she says. "And on a hot summer's day. It's almost noon."

"I don't have a choice," I say. I don't look away from the computer screen, my fingers still moving across the keyboard, the grey curtains half-drawn and my pale face bathed in fluorescent light. "I have to get this finished."

"You're obsessed," she says.

"I'm not obsessed; I'm just focused," I say pointing to the screen and the stack of papers next to my empty coffee cup. "The going is good, and I need to finish my work before it slips away."

"I think you're being selfish," she says.

I don't say anything.

She closes the office door, but we both know she's right.

I like the idea of focusing on a single idea for hours at a time, but when I talk about focus, it's the shiny side of the coin, the side I show to the world.

I considered calling this chapter "Focus On a Single Idea," but that would have been a sanitised version of what I'm about to tell you.

Focus is a clean and easy word that I feel at home talking in public about. The other side of the coin, the side of obsession, is grubbier to look at, but don't mistake its value. It's what will help you finish.

Beyond Sense or Reason

Three weeks.

That's how long it took American author, Jack Kerouac (1922-1969) to write the first draft of his beat novel *On the Road*.

Kerouac was so obsessed with his idea for a post-war road-trip novel that he typed his manuscript single-spaced without margins or paragraph breaks.

He fuelled himself up on amphetamines and coffee at the time, but what Kerouac put into his writing (or what he poisoned his body with) isn't the kind of obsession I'm describing.

What people leave out from this story is that Kerouac obsessed about his idea afterwards, and he spent another five years editing that manuscript before it was published.

The story of writing a manuscript in a hot three-week burst of creativity appeals to those who want a quick fix or a shortcut, but almost all real, lasting, creative work is harder and more time-consuming than anything you can achieve in three short weeks.

Be obsessed.

Because it's hard. You get in from a day of grinding out widgets, stacking shelves or pushing numbers from one spreadsheet to the next. Your back aches, and you want nothing more for the day than to sit on the couch and bathe in the warm glow of easy television.

This is so much easier than going back at it. I deserve to relax. Why should I bother with more work?

When you're called to account, you can point to the reality television programmes you watched and the hours you spent looking at photos of somebody else's sanitised life on Facebook.

Or you can point to the ideas you stuck with and to what you created, even when everybody said you were wasting your time. You can show what you created when nobody expected it.

Be obsessed.

I get up most mornings before 06:00 a.m. I meditate for 20 minutes, brew strong, sweet coffee, and then I sit at my desk for two hours until it's time to get my kids up for school. Afterwards, I drive my 20-year-old Toyota Corolla through heavy traffic and across Dublin city to work.

My morning routine doesn't turn me into a better person. I don't even like getting up early; what fun is 05:00 a.m. when you've had six hours' sleep, and you're missing a warm bed?

I'd much rather write into the wee small hours after midnight with music playing quietly, nowhere to go tomorrow and no one to please. But I do it in the morning.

I do it because if I don't turn up first thing, the day will take what creative energy I have away from me.

An hour sitting behind a hundred cars on lane two of the motorway, a job to handle, 1,000 emails, conference phone calls, overdue deadlines, meetings about meetings, getting paid, getting promoted, getting fired, a semblance of a career, balancing the budget, not having enough, two kids, a neglected wife, manic thoughts in the supermarket, a dinner to prepare, clean up after or be grateful for, TV, Netflix, Facebook, Twitter, a crappy WiFi connection, a leaky shower, light bulbs to change, friends to meet and more.

I'm forgetting about late night pints of Guinness and then an aching head, and then me with nothing left, not turning up and creative work going undone. There is always tomorrow.

There is only today.

On the good mornings, when the rising sun slips in through cracks of my Venetian office blinds, the words and ideas come quickly. My fingers move across the keyboard; I'm playing the piano.

On the bad mornings, when I'm shivering and longing for the duvet in the other room, I sit at my desk, fiddle with the chair, and I open up Word or Scrivener.

The flashing black cursor and the blank page terrify me. It's expecting the momentum of my idea to propel it across the screen and fill the empty white page with black.

"Don't look at me like that," I say. "I've got nothing."

The blank cursor just blinks.

I bang my head off the wooden desk and nurse my cooling coffee. Then, I force myself to press my fingers on the keyboard, to move the boulder an inch up the hill and keep going until it's time to stop.

It's my job to do the same again tomorrow. And the day after that. All that matters is that I turn up.

Extreme Measures

In 1830, French poet and novelist Victor Hugo (1802-1885) was in trouble. The previous year, he had agreed with his publisher that he would write a new book called *Notre-Dame de Paris*.

There was just one problem.

Like a lot of successful artists, Hugo procrastinated on writing his new book. He spent a year entertaining guests, getting involved in the politics of the day, and doing anything but his most important work. To compound matters, Hugo even lost a critical notebook containing his research for the book. Perhaps Hugo was afraid of lasting success?

His publisher didn't care. They demanded Hugo finish his book by February of 1831, giving the procrastinating author just five-and-a-half months to write his novel, which is a difficult deadline even by today's standards.

Hugo grew despondent about his lack of progress, but instead of quitting, he put an extreme plan into action. He gathered his clothes and locked them away, keeping only a large grey woollen garment and a bottle of ink. The lack of suitable outdoor clothing forced Hugo to stay indoors and write his book.

Hugo stayed in his study each day and wrote. He left his desk only to eat and sleep and to speak to friends who came to visit him in the evenings.

Adele Foucher, Hugo's wife, wrote,

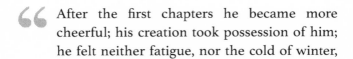 After the first chapters he became more cheerful; his creation took possession of him; he felt neither fatigue, nor the cold of winter,

which had come; in December he worked
with open windows."

Hugo's obsessive creative strategy succeeded. *Notre-Dame de Paris* or *Hunchback of Notre Dame* was published two weeks early on January 14, 1831.

If there's one lesson from Hugo's way of creating, it's that great work demands an extreme level of focus from the artist.

Many aspiring artists today lead lives of quiet distraction, and they can't afford to lock themselves away like Victor Hugo for six months.

Even if you could, you'd still face television, the internet and a 1,000 other digital distractions that artists of the past couldn't imagine.

Instead, focus your external resources on your creative work and reduce or remove anything that distracts you. Marshall your free money and time towards your most important creative work and commit entirely to your creative project. Postpone or cancel everything you can get away with.

When you do this, you'll see every decision you face through the gaze of your creative work, and you will ask: "How does this move my work forward?"

You can focus your inner resources – your cognitive attention and energy – on your most important work by turning off, disconnecting, disabling and unsubscribing from whatever you can.

All that matters is that you give your ideas what they need to bond with each other.

Put aside your thoughts of material goods or personal image, if only for a while, because these thoughts will do nothing more than sap the limited mental energy you need to create.

Obsessed artists (or at least the ones we're interested in) don't spend hours shopping on Amazon or wandering around the local supermarket while their creative work remains undone.

Yes, it's natural and sometimes even productive to procrastinate about your big idea, but you must start. You must create.

You must finish.

On the Hunt

Because you're obsessed, you know anybody who says, "I've got no great ideas; I can't think of anything to say," isn't doing their most important work. They've quit before the end of the race.

You don't quit without an idea. You are a collector of ideas and a thief. It's in your nature to do more than just read, listen or consume other people's works. You can't amble from one day or one idea to the next like a vagabond without purpose or principle.

You make use of everything.

The fine sentences you discover in a book of Raymond Carver's poetry, the texture of the medium-rare fillet steak you eat for dinner, an early morning drizzle against your bedroom window, your nose to the ground sniffing the dirt for ideas, a print of *La Musique* hanging next to where you write, a story you find about Victor Hugo, an interview with J.K. Rowling, when your wife said you are selfish, the time they fired you for a basic mathematical error, your naked ambition, the biographies of your betters, the critic who hates your work and worse: those who ignore it.

All of it goes in.

It's a melting pot, and all that matters is the result.

Be obsessed.

When you show others what you've done, somebody will say,

"That isn't very good. Who do you think you are to say such a thing?"

Ignore them.

British author, J.K. Rowling (b. 1965), obsessed about becoming a writer since she was six years old.

After she graduated university with a degree, her marriage broke down, she lost her job and later, she was diagnosed with clinical depression. A single mother, living on benefits, Rowling couldn't even afford to pay her rent of £600.

"We're talking suicidal thoughts here, we're not talking 'I'm a little bit miserable,'" Rowling said.

Rowling sought help for depression, and she did the work. Instead of locking her clothes away like Hugo, she wrote *Harry Potter and the Philosopher's Stone* using pen and paper in cafés around Edinburgh.

Rowling didn't worry about her tools or her way of working; she obsessed about her big idea.

She also wrote the early drafts of her book on an old typewriter, and if she wanted to change a paragraph, she had to retype the entire page. Later, Rowling even retyped the entire book because it wasn't double-spaced (an industry-standard format for writers submitting their work to editors and agents).

When Rowling posted the finished manuscript to a literary agent, he sent Rowling back a slip saying, "My list is full. The folder you sent wouldn't fit in the envelope."

The second agent Rowling contacted had more foresight.

Creativity is sometimes messy.

Bleed into Your Work

Caution: obsession will spill into other areas of your life.

I spent the second half of 2015, running 30-to-40 miles a week. I was training for the Dublin City Marathon.

One weekend in September and six weeks out from race day, I set out to run 18 miles down the bank of the Grand Canal in Dublin. I was struggling with a chest infection, and it hurt to breathe. Twelve miles in, my paced slowed and my head began to spin. Finally, I turned around and walked home.

That walk haunted me all week.

Creativity is sometimes messy

Even though I knew I was sick and common sense demanded I stop, I felt worried. If I couldn't even finish a simple long-distance training run, how was I going to run 26.2 miles on race day?

The following Saturday morning with my chest infection gone, I got up at 05:30 a.m., put on my white trainers and set out on the road for another 18 miles. I was stronger, more clear-headed and faster than before.

I reached the same stretch of the Grand Canal when I felt the bulge of my rapidly filling bladder. So, I stopped at a bush off the beaten track, undid my shorts and urinated blood into the ditch.

I ran on for another three miles before admitting to myself that I had to stop.

(I found out much later this wasn't blood; it was excess unprocessed protein in my system, which is a common ailment of long-distance runners.)

On the day of the race, I felt healthy, fit and even fast. Or at least I did until I reached mile 21. By then, my legs and arms felt like acid was pumping through them, my stomach tightened, and I felt dizzy and unsure of where I was.

I thought of pulling off the side of the road, of sitting down on the ground and of doing the easy thing.

Instead, I stared at the back of a tall, athletic man with greying hair running ahead of me. He was waving to the crowds holding signs and handing out oranges and jellies, and he looked more comfortable and confident than I'd felt at mile five.

I thought of blood on the side of the canal, of wasted time and effort, of going through 12 months with the memory of a race I gave up on, of how I didn't want it badly enough.

I gritted my teeth, matched the man's pace and focused on the black and white numbers 62307 pinned to the back of his red running singlet.

Together we ran, neither of us particularly fast, me sweating, swearing and shaking and him waving and smiling. We ran past those other runners who stopped to walk, sit down or quit.

They just didn't want it badly enough.

The two of us were 500 metres from the finish line when the man's right knee buckled. He collapsed to the concrete, roared like a wounded animal and drew his right knee to his chest.

The stewards ran across the track, picked him off the ground and carried my companion away from the finish line and towards the medic bay. His great race, undone.

I ran on.

I ran over the line.

Be obsessed. Know that you're not done when you think you are.

You release your idea into the world; you sit back and wait and then . . . people do worse than criticise your work.

They ignore it.

Your heart cracks at the wasted time, effort, and disappointment. You feel like a failure, and that life would be so much easier if you didn't have to do this hot, white creative thing. You think of stopping, of giving up, of doing what's easy.

You forget that the work itself is the lesson and the reward. You forget until you pick yourself up from the dirt and put one foot in front of the other. You go back at it. You go back at it, hard.

Because you're obsessed.

Creative Takeaways

- Pick one idea to obsess about until it's done. Work on nothing else.
- When you face a question of how to spend your limited money or time, ask "Does this decision advance my big idea?"

5

ROOT OUT PERFECTIONISM LIKE
A WEED

*"Remember that, sooner or later, before it ever reaches perfection,
you will have to let it go and move on and start to write the next
thing. Perfection is like chasing the horizon. Keep moving."*
– Neil Gaiman

When I was in my mid-twenties, I wanted to create award-winning literary fiction. I looked at the Christy Browns, Anne Enrights and Colm Tóibíns of the world (all award-winning Irish literary authors), and I thought, "Why not me?"

Behold my ego.

Bear with me, because it gets worse.

I knew I had to improve at my craft – and fast. Along with 15 other aspiring writers, I enrolled in an intensive creative writing and nonfiction writing class in the Irish Writers' Centre in Dublin.

For a year, we met every Monday evening in an airy

room on the first floor of a Georgian town house on the north side of the city. We spent two hours critiquing each others' work, discussing literary fiction and nonfiction and pretending like we knew what we were talking about.

Our tutor was a balding American in his early thirties from Texas, and we listened to him talk about literature, a great sentence, and the job of a writer for two hours before going to the pub.

I don't think our tutor liked us very much – he once compared teaching us about writing to "feeding lions at the zoo" – but I didn't care.

The man knew his craft, even if we were beneath it.

He encouraged us to highlight sentences we liked, to write on the margins of the books we loved and seek out the writer's holy grail: one fine sentence that reveals an essential truth about life.

Our tutor wanted us not to just read great literature, but to get black ink beneath our fingernails, breathe it in and ask the creative master before us, "How do you move people with a big idea?"

Our job was to do more than admire great literature; we had to drown in it.

Each night after class, the tutor, my classmates (would-be Irish writers in their 20s, 30s and 40s), and I went to a pub five minutes from the Irish Writers' Centre. We drank pitchers of cheap beer, talked about Ernest Hemingway, Neil Gaiman and Anne Enright until the bar closed.

My tutor was fresh from a recent divorce, and he was more concerned with getting the phone numbers of the female students than anything I had to say or write, but one night I caught his attention.

"Jeff," I said. "I'm struggling to finish this idea I have for a story, but it's too damn hard. What do I need to do to write something great?"

"Bryan, your writing is full of clichés," he said stroking his goatee. "You write like a 1920s pulp fiction novelist."

"I can work on that," I said. "Tell me how I can write a really great sentence. Is there a devil I can make a deal with?"

"Trying to write one true great sentence is like throwing a typewriter at the moon."

I sipped my beer. "What do you mean?"

"It's impossible."

We laughed, but I didn't listen to him.

I spent my free time after work and on the weekends writing and rewriting the same sentences, printing them out, reading them aloud and rewriting my essays and short stories repeatedly.

I threw typewriters at the moon for about four years (long after the class finished), and in that time, I finished just six short stories. These stories had pretty sentences, but here's the painful truth:

They were lousy.

They were overwritten, pretentious and worst of all, boring.

I was so consumed by my quest for the perfect sentence that I forgot great stories (the ones by writers like Enright and Gaiman) succeed because of the tale and the characters within in them and not just because the writer arranges the verbs, nouns, adjectives and adverbs in the right order.

That wasn't the worst part either.

Because I'd failed to finish a lot of my stories, it was almost impossible for me to get candid real-world feedback about the quality of my writing. Six short stories aren't much to show after four years of work.

My pursuit of perfectionism almost choked the life out of the part of me that loves to write.

Dangerous Perfectionist Traits

Perfectionism is indulgent, selfish and sometimes tragic. You work on an idea for a time and draw towards the finish line.

Then you pull back, deciding your idea isn't ready. You put your head down and work on without getting any critical feedback. Your lack of apparent progress is frustrating, so you decide the only solution is to work harder.

Because you avoid releasing your work into the world, your audience never sees what you're working on. You don't get the chance to use what they tell you to create something new, something better.

The weeds of perfectionism grow around the root of your idea and choke the life out of whatever creative resources you have left.

Finally, spent and broken, you give up on your big idea altogether, but there is a better way. You just need to figure out the kinds of perfectionism holding you back and then root out this personality trait from your creative life. Because I want you to avoid my mistakes, you must watch for the following traits:

The *tool-hungry* perfectionist waits until he is in a perfect environment. He looks for the right tools like a cutting-edge computer, an oak desk, a large white room, unopened supplies, clean and crisp paper and all he needs before he gets to work. He waits and waits, and he never begins.

The *lacking* perfectionist insists on having enough funding and time to work on his great idea: a grant, a sabbatical, a year off and an apartment in Paris; only then can he start. The money and the day never come.

The *uninspired* perfectionist insists on finding the perfect idea before she invests herself and her resources in her work. She waits until inspiration strikes her in a dream, when she takes the dog for a walk, while cooking dinner, going to the gym and watching television. She waits and waits, but inspiration never arrives.

The *impossible* perfectionist holds himself and his idea to an impossible standard. He insists on creative excellence, and his work is never good enough. He always has more to do.

Have you met the *obsessive-compulsive* perfectionist?

She insists on getting every detail right because the devil is in the details. The font on her book cover isn't quite right, the colours of her album cover don't look good enough from a distance, and her film title isn't memorable enough. She works long after sense and reason have departed and straight through every deadline.

The *greedy* perfectionist spends hours cramming more research, arguments, stories, layers and ideas into his work so it'll be that bit more credible. He lies awake at night afraid that the minimum version of his idea will be criticised as flimsy or shoddy. He needs more than his peers and more than his competitors. It's never enough.

The *tinkering* perfectionist picks over every small detail, second-guesses all of her creative decisions and constantly changes what she's created. She wonders if she should put in X, take out Y and rework Z. As she tinkers, her idea falls apart.

The *never-ready* perfectionist waits until his work is finished before he shows it to anyone. He works for hours, days, weeks, months and years at a time (and almost always alone), and he never shows anyone what he's created because it's not ready. He never finishes.

Proven Strategies for Overcoming Perfectionism

If you are a *tool-hungry* perfectionist, here's food for thought.

Irish writer Christy Brown (1932-1981) was born with cerebral palsy into a large working class family in Dublin. Brown's disability confined him to a wheelchair, and his family didn't have much money or resources to provide what he needed, but he didn't care.

Christy painted and wrote novels by pressing a paintbrush or pencil between the toes of his left foot or by using his left foot to type on an old typewriter.

The *lacking* perfectionist can learn a lesson from Brown's life too.

Having enough tools, money and time is nice, but a lack of resources shouldn't interfere with your creative process. Instead, use what you lack to confine your ideas or your work and give it structure.

If you're an *uninspired* perfectionist, remember that sitting around all day, drinking coffee and waiting for inspiration to ring your doorbell means nothing gets done. If you do this for weeks or months, you'll never finish, and the artist who never finishes isn't a professional.

Instead of waiting for inspiration to strike, seek new ideas every day in the books you read, music you listen to and people you meet. Write down what you find, and use what you learn almost immediately in your work.

If you're an *impossible* or *obsessive* perfectionist, accept that perfection is an elusive and even a dangerous goal.

While it's important to do your work to a high standard, it's better to ship it because then your ideas can help other people. Even if your ideas flop, releasing them from your head makes room for new, better ideas.

Are you a *greedy perfectionist*?

Create a clear plan for how long you will spend researching your ideas and set a date for moving from the research phase to the creation phase. Yes, reading one more book, completing one more interview or finding one more idea could help, but sometimes the real discovery lies in the making. And you're on the hook for it.

If you're a *procrastinating perfectionist*, spend 15 minutes today reviewing your calendar and planning how long you intend to spend on your work over the next one to three months.

Instead of abandoning a creative project or slaving away indefinitely, set a target for submission or publication. Stick to this target and, if you miss it, finish, publish or submit your work as soon as you can.

Are you a *tinkering perfectionist?*

Narrow your focus.

When you have too many different ideas on the go at once, you'll either overload your work or burn out. Instead, focus on the parts of your idea that matter today and finish those.

If you're a *never-ready perfectionist*, show your work to a friend, a family member or a professional you admire and ask them for frank and candid feedback. There's no need to ship mediocrity for the sake of it; just don't let your project sit indefinitely in a drawer.

Once you've rooted out these perfectionist personality traits, you'll start to find more mistakes in the work you show to others, but that's OK. You can learn from these mistakes like the creative masters at Pixar.

Learning from a Cowboy's Big Mistake

Sheriff Woody Pride didn't always play nice.

In 1992, John Lasseter (b. 1957) and the creative team behind *Toy Story* struggled to create a version of Woody that worked. Studio executives at the time felt the earlier versions of Woody were too earnest, perky and unbelievable. They wanted a Woody with more "edge."

The creative team at Pixar listened to the executive team's advice, but they went too far. They transformed their easy-going if unbelievable cowboy into a dark and mean bully.

There's a scene in *Toy Story* where Woody knocks his friend Buzz Lightyear out a bedroom window by accident, but this darker and more aggressive Woody threw Buzz out the window for spite.

When Lasseter and his team showed this new version of Woody to Disney executives, they were horrified. This bully was supposed to be a hero of the film, but he wasn't a character kids could love.

Lasseter calls what happened next "Black Friday."

The executives shut the production down, and the film's future was put in jeopardy.

The creative team spent another year working on the *Toy Story* script to figure out how to overcome their mistakes, return Woody to his roots and create a believable and balanced character that would appeal to younger and older audiences alike.

Finally, the found the heart of the movie – a cowboy

who wanted to be loved – by trusting their storytelling instincts after falling down along the way.

Lasseter and the other creative masters at Pixar would have never completed *Toy Story* and its even more popular sequels if they hadn't used their early mistakes as learning opportunities, as a way of trusting their natural storytelling instincts.

In *Creativity Inc.*, Ed Catmull, the president of Pixar Animation Studios, explains,

 The *Toy Story* team knew and trusted each other – over the years, they'd made stupid mistakes together and solved seemingly insurmountable problems together."

Like the creative masters at Pixar, trust yourself to make stupid mistakes and accept them for what they are: signs you're doing the hard work. On the other hand, the artist who gives into their fears about mistakes allows perfectionism to choke the life from their big idea.

What if John Lasseter and his team had given up on Woody because they'd gotten things wrong first time around? What if they'd avoided doing the hard thing, of showing their idea to others? What if they hadn't used early feedback to ultimately improve their creation?

Toy Story would have been shelved, never seeing completion.

Reframing Your Mistakes

Writers often send early versions of their books to readers, while musicians try out early versions of new songs at live shows and release EPs and singles before letting a new album out into the world.

If you're uncomfortable with releasing early versions of your work to a wider audience, at least reveal your ideas to an inner circle of beta readers, early listeners or first customers.

When your big idea pushes its way out of the earth and into the world for others to see, congratulate yourself. It's important to mark these creative wins, however small.

Some people might criticise, reject or even ignore your flowering idea, and they could be right. After a few days or weeks, review how your audience received your big idea. Is your big idea unbelievable? Is your "Woody"' too dark?

Root out the choking weeds and then craft a plan for avoiding your mistakes in future versions of your idea. By adopting this approach, you can transform your unbelievable or mean-spirited Woody into a creation your audience loves.

Look, nobody likes when others point out their mistakes or even when a big idea fails. It's not acceptable to give up on excellence or ship derivative creative works, but you must stop measuring what you create against an impossible standard.

Typos, unclear points, badly written stories and articles nobody wants to read keep me up at night, but mistakes are the dirty secret behind every creative act.

You must get comfortable with things failing to take root. It's part of the creative process, and it's not a reflection on your talents or lack thereof. I hate rereading old published pieces of writing. I spot sentences that don't flow, points I didn't back up sufficiently and stories where I wasn't honest enough.

In the end, I felt awful about this lack of progress, I

didn't get the valuable feedback writers need from readers and editors, and I gave up.

Instead of doing the work, of coming up with new ideas, I concentrated on getting better at games like *Call of Duty*.

I got pretty good too.

Hey, computer games are more fun than trying to fill a blank page.

One dark Wednesday night in January, I lost an epic battle of *Call of Duty* to a team of fifteen-year-old Americans.

I put down my Xbox controller and picked up a book about Leonardo da Vinci. There, I found this quote: "Art is never finished, only abandoned."

Something clicked.

I realised there's no such thing as the perfect idea. So what if it's not perfect? It's not meant to be perfect.

The more I read, the more I discovered that creative masters – like da Vinci, Tharp, McCartney and Dali – don't ever find a perfect idea, they pick ONE idea, they work on it day in and day out and see it through.

So I gave my Xbox to my son and decided to finish writing a book and a collection of short stories. I committed to learning as much as I could about writing and seeing each idea through, even if they were terrible.

Even today my instinct is almost always to put down the old piece of writing and never look at it again. Instead, I force myself to assess how I can avoid committing the mistakes I find in the next thing I write. I finish what I started, and then I move on. You should too.

Typewriters and the moon be damned.

Creative Takeaways

- Identify the perfectionist traits holding you back and craft a plan for rooting them out from your creative life.
- Show what you created to someone outside of your immediate circle and ask them for candid feedback. Celebrate. Because today, this is your small victory.

6

PRACTISE YOUR CRAFT DELIBERATELY

"In fact, researchers have settled on what they believe is the magic number for true expertise: ten thousand hours."
– Malcolm Gladwell

How long did you practise your craft today AND how did it go?

Swedish psychologist K. Anders Ericsson, whom I introduced in Chapter 3, lays out a bold case for how long it takes to master a discipline like writing, painting or playing the violin (a case popularised by Malcolm Gladwell in *Outliers*).

According to Ericsson, it takes approximately 10,000 hours of practise to master a discipline like playing the violin or writing.

Several years ago, I wanted to achieve my 10,000 hours. So I set a target of writing just fiction for three hours a day, every day.

I picked three hours a day because most fiction writers – even Stephen King – don't write more than three hours a day, every day. I recorded how long I spent writing fiction each morning, using a timer on my computer, and I totalled up the hours at the end of the week.

Three hours a day adds up to 21 hours a week and approximately 1,000 hours a year. At this rate, it would take at least 10 years to achieve mastery, provided I wrote seven days a week, 365 days a year.

No sick days, no holidays, and no time off.

I found it impossible to balance the demands of a job and family life with my 10,000 hours goal. I resented my lack of progress, and my plan fell apart within weeks. Then I discovered how Mozart turned deliberate practise into part of his early life.

The Origins of Mozart

Austrian composer Wolfgang Amadeus Mozart (1756-1791) practised in obscurity for a mere 13 years (or more than 10,000 hours) before developing a style of his own and becoming popular.

Under his father Leopold's guidance, the boy-genius learnt to play the piano, the clarinet, the violin and other musical instruments. He also learnt how to compose music. Leopold Mozart recognised his son's early talents and even believed he was a divine gift.

With his father, Wolfgang studied the great music of the day. He travelled to the courts of France, Austria, Germany and England to perform alongside other musicians. He also emulated the popular musical styles of composers he met.

In London between 1764 and 1765, Mozart spent two years practising his craft under the guidance of Johann Christian Bach, the eleventh son of Johann Sebastian Bach.

During a concert on May 19, 1764, Bach took Mozart onto his lap and according to a witness:

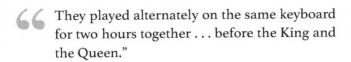 They played alternately on the same keyboard for two hours together . . . before the King and the Queen."

Mozart imitated Bach's playing style and discussed music at length with him. Today, musical scholars have drawn a strong link between some of Mozart's and Bach's works.

As he grew older, Mozart continued to play music, work with other composers and deliberately practise each area of his craft. In doing this, he more quickly discovered where his true talents lay.

He realised he wasn't a musician; he was a *composer*. He also decided his future didn't lie in playing church music in Salzburg for Archbishop Colloredo.

The Archbishop had little time for Mozart's desires to compose, instead preferring Mozart played music for the people of Vienna.

So Mozart wrote to his estranged father who by now was dependent on Mozart for financial income.

I am a composer . . . I neither can nor ought to bury the talent for composition with which God in his goodness has so richly endowed me."

Then Mozart spent the remainder of his life working towards one goal: becoming a great composer.

The Problem with Mindless Practise

Mozart is an extreme example of a creative master. He possessed enough innate talents to deliberately practise his craft as a young boy at a level normally reserved for adults.

So while Mozart's experience does not directly correlate with that of your typical creative, you can still learn from him.

Although Mozart was a musical genius, the trajectory of his artistic career demonstrates that the quality of time you spend practising your craft is as important as the quantity. He worked hard at perfecting his skills and played or composed almost every day for his entire life.

Understand that creativity is also more unpredictable than simple mathematics. The famous "10,000 Hour Rule" refers to everything creative people do, not just the time you spend with a violin or a pen in your hand. Putting in your time won't have the impact you want if you aren't doing so deliberately.

It's inadvisable to put the hours in each day at your desk or in the studio if you're unaware of how this practise will progress your craft. Similarly, you're wasting your time if you don't evaluate your performance and get critical feedback from others about your work.

If you practise your craft each day without experiencing real progress, this creative stagnation will inevitably reduce confidence in your abilities. It's either that or you'll find the process of doing the same thing day-in, day-out boring and eventually look for more exciting things to pursue.

Accomplished violinist and academic Noa Kageyama specialises in helping talented musicians audition for orchestras, and he also sits on the board at the Juilliard

School in New York. He describes his experiences of mind-less practise:

 I remember struggling with the left-hand pizzicato variation in Paganini's 24th Caprice when I was studying at Juilliard. I kept trying harder and harder to make the notes speak, but all I got was sore fingers, a couple of which actually started to bleed (well, just a tiny bit)."

That was one of my mistakes. I kept trying to write the same stories, and all I got were rejection letters and failed competition entries. I was too focused on fiction writing, and I didn't count other types of writing, like blogging or copywriting, as counting toward my practise. I also didn't count the time I spent studying topics, like creativity and storytelling as practise.

If a weightlifter lifts the same weights in the gym each day, their body will adapt, and if they continue to mindlessly practise lifting weights, they'll never become stronger.

If you want the bond between your ideas to grow stronger and more powerful, you must increase the demands upon yourself and your work.

You too must avoid mindless practise if you want to master your chosen discipline. Beware of penning the same stories, drawing the same pictures or playing the same songs each night.

The S-Shaped Curve of Creativity

The S-shaped curve of creativity represents the trajectory of creative output over time and your mastery over elements of your craft. As you invest more hours into your discipline, you will move further along this curve.

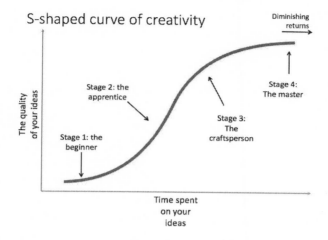

The S-shaped curve of creativity

The *first stage* of the S-shaped curve belongs to the beginner, to the outsider. Here, you invest a significant amount of time and resources and for negligible returns.

Like young Mozart, you imitate, copy others and look to the Bachs of your craft for advice.

Unless you possess his genius, it's natural to think the quality of your creative output is low or derivative. If you're a writer, you'll pen dozens of stories that are abandoned, rejected or end up in the bin.

If you're a musician, you'll compose bar after bar and then discard them. If you're a filmmaker, you'll storyboard idea after idea for your film without ever shooting a scene that belongs in the final cut.

You might feel discouraged by your lack of progress and wonder if practising in obscurity is worth it.

Persevere!

Spend more time deliberately practising your craft and you will reach the second stage of the S-shaped curve of creativity.

As an apprentice, you feel more comfortable with your medium of choice, the task at hand and what you want to achieve. You're able to scale your creative ideas in quantity and quality too.

You finish a book, record an album or release a short film that you feel confident about showing to your peers. You're an outsider, unburdened by the curse of knowledge. You can approach your craft in a fresh and exciting way.

In Mozart's case, as a teenager, he began to write compositions that alarmed his father because they were too complicated and different from the popular music of the day.

At the *third stage* of the S-shaped curve, your voice is stronger and more confident and your style distinct. As a craftsperson, it's natural sometimes to experience setbacks and even feel discouraged about how far you have to go to master your craft.

In Mozart's case, he faced many setbacks.

One came during a trip to Paris in 1777 when he was 17. Despite his obvious skill, Mozart struggled to find a job that matched his talents.

After his mother died, he was in need of money. So he returned to Salzburg. There, he took up a position working under Archbishop Colloredo as the court's organist and as keyboard instructor for aristocratic children.

Although he felt confident about his abilities, Mozart felt trapped by his father, the job and his new boss.

If you're luckier than Mozart, a supportive outside expert will help you work through this stage. Your editor, producer or creative mentor can provide you with an outside view of your performances or work to date. With their help, you can push past your inevitable setbacks.

The *final point* of the S-shaped curve of creativity comes when you have mastered your craft, or an element of it. You're able to express your voice and your ideas in a way that compels others to listen. And you know how it feels to finish working on an idea that succeeds.

While it might take just a few weeks or months to master an element, mastery over your craft as a whole could take a lifetime.

In other words, you could practise playing a song on a guitar and reach the final point of the S-shaped curve in your mastery of a song, while at the same time finding yourself at the first point of this curve in your abilities as a musician.

Mozart mastered his craft in his mid-twenties. After composing the opera *Idomeneo*, which premiered in Munich in 1781, he broke from the archbishop and his father and moved to an apartment in Vienna. Finally free, he composed great works like the *Haydn Quartets* and *The Marriage of Figaro*.

How to Deliberately Practise Your Craft

To deliberately practise your craft, you must push yourself in new and exciting directions. This effort is slower, more tedious and painful than mindless practise, but it will help you avoid diminishing returns.

Kageyama wrote:

 Deliberate, or mindful practise is a systematic
and highly structured activity, that is, for lack
of a better word, more scientific. Instead of
mindless trial and error, it is an active and
thoughtful process of hypothesis testing
where we relentlessly seek solutions to clearly
defined problems."

You must be open to new ideas, even when you're not
sitting at your desk, in the studio or in front of the blank
page. Study creative masters in your subject of choice (as
Mozart did with Bach), use what you discover to improve
your craft and commit to a lifelong study of your chosen
discipline.

Here's how you can put in your 10,000 hours of practise
without trial and error.

1. Set a Target

You must exercise your craft over and over so that it
becomes subconscious but not unfocused. To avoid mindless practise, set a challenging target for each of your
sessions this week and this month.

For example, your goal for today's deliberate practise
session could be to perform the opening note of a solo piece
or to write an introduction for your book. When it's time to
practise, focus only on this target. Tomorrow, pick a different
but equally specific target.

Setting the aim for your practise sessions will give you
confines in which to practise and something tangible to
reach. It will also help you apply your creative energies to

specific areas of your craft, and as your deliberate sessions stack up on top of each other, you'll accomplish more over time.

2. Focus Relentlessly on Reaching Your Targets

Mozart was at his desk every morning by 07:00 a.m. to compose.

You too must eliminate superfluous activities and anything that distracts you from the task at hand so that you can deliberately practise for 30 to 90 minutes, alone and without interruption.

Beware, too, of trying to accomplish more than one thing at once. The productive gains of multi-tasking are a myth and attempting to write, paint or draw while checking email, talking to others and considering what you want to cook for dinner will stagnate your progress.

If you attempt to perform two tasks at the same time, understand that you can't do both at once. Instead, your brain rapidly switches from one task to the other. If you have to stop and think about just one of these tasks, you'll slow down at both.

In the end, you reduce the benefits of deliberate practice and exhaust your limited mental resources faster.

3. Time and Track Yourself

Creative people often feel uncomfortable with the "right brain" thinking that goes with self-quantification, but it's hard to argue with cold maths.

Remember, what gets measured gets managed, and what gets managed gets done. If you're a professional creative, then you're in the business of getting things done.

Timing the length of your practise will help you become more realistic about the amount of time you spend doing the work.

According to the *Paris Review*, Ernest Hemingway (1899-1961) recorded his daily word count on a large chart. He kept it beneath a mounted gazelle head near where he wrote "so as not to kid myself."

Record in a journal or spreadsheet the amount of time you write, draw, paint or play. Like Hemingway, keep a running tally so as not to fool yourself. This self-knowledge will help you identify when you are working hard but achieving little.

4. Troubleshoot, Iterate and Repeat

If you set a challenging target, you may not hit it on the first, second or even on the tenth go. The trick is to critically analyse what's holding you back from progressing. Be brutally honest with yourself.

Ask, "Where did I go wrong?" and, "What held me back?" Then use your answers to improve the manner in which you deliberately practise.

When Kageyama encounters difficulties while deliberately practising the violin, he pauses to reflect on how his practise is going and what he can do to improve.

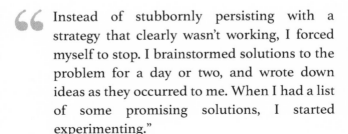 Instead of stubbornly persisting with a strategy that clearly wasn't working, I forced myself to stop. I brainstormed solutions to the problem for a day or two, and wrote down ideas as they occurred to me. When I had a list of some promising solutions, I started experimenting."

I used his advice to adapt how I write. For example, I regularly come across new hooks for stories and ways of writing better sentences. I record these religiously in a creative notebook and review them often.

You too can avoid playing or practising from memory by writing down the lessons you've learnt about your craft and then using these insights to inform future practise sessions.

How Accountability Helps

Have you worked on a project and faced internal resistance, but when you're put in charge of the project, you take ownership of it and your internal resistance dissolves?

A creative accountability partner will help you take ownership over your craft and deliberately practise. Turn to a friend, a family member or a peer in a writing group or band.

It's helpful if your accountability partner is working on a creative project too, as they are more likely to understand the process and what it feels like to be doing the work.

Their role is to check in with you regularly – once a day, a week, a month or as often as is necessary – to see how your work is progressing.

This check-in could be something as simple as a conversation where you say, "I completed a film sequence this week."

Often, simply knowing you have to tell someone how you are getting on is enough to overcome procrastination and focus on your creative work.

With the support of an accountability partner, you're less likely to break your commitment and stop practising if they encourage you to push through the difficult patches.

The Essential Role of Critical Feedback

Critical feedback about your work will help you move along the S-shaped curve of creativity faster.

Bashing out a 50,000-page novel and then asking your mother, father or favourite aunt to read it and tell you that your novel is the "the next big thing" isn't useful. Instead, show your work to someone more accomplished than you and ask them to evaluate it coldly and ruthlessly.

If you're a new writer, for example, get critical feedback on your work by hiring an editor to read what you've written and give you a frank evaluation on where you need to improve.

If you're a musician, pay a more talented player or hire a producer to listen to your work and then explain where you need to practice. If you're an artist, attend a class and ask the teacher to comment on your paintings.

Be Smart, Be Patient

Today, Mozart is hailed as a "genius of geniuses," but it's worth remembering that even he deliberately practised his craft for 13 years before he produced popular works of his own. He had to perfect his musical style, and he did so by relying on the guidance of mentors like Bach.

There are no shortcuts to creative success, even for Mozart. If you're ready to practise your craft for 13 or even 30 years, be smart about it.

Work on improving the elements that you're weakest at doing; get outside help if you need to. Seek out other creative masters you admire (whether living or dead), and draw out lessons that you can use to improve your skills.

Set yourself targets for each of your practise sessions

and, at least once a week, ask yourself how you're progressing and what you can do to improve.

Because it all counts.

Creative Takeaways

- Reflect on your routine for practising your creative work. Now ask yourself is it mindless or deliberate?
- Prepare your four-step plan for deliberately practising your craft.

7

CUT THE CORD

"We must do our work for its own sake, not for fortune or attention or applause."
– Steven Pressfield

In this chapter, I was going to share a step-by-step guide of how you learn to do the work and become more creative.

Instead, I want to do something different. I am going to share a personal story so that you can see how I learnt to do the work.

Why?

Well, what's worse than knowing exactly what you must do but failing to act? Why go to the bother of figuring out your path and setting goals if you don't do the work to move forward?

I want you to burn up like a good bonfire (see book 1) and leave no trace of yourself behind. Let your work consume you entirely. And then when you have finished, you'll look back and wonder, "How did I do that?"

So, let me take you back to my life in 2005...

My girlfriend walked out of my parent's ensuite, pale and clenching a pregnancy test stick.

"I didn't think it would be positive."

I did. A month and a half ago we'd capped off a boozy weekend away at a wedding by checking into a B&B just miles from home. We relied on the morning after pill for protection – apparently, it becomes less effective each time you use it – and when she told me she was late, I knew.

The second pregnancy test agreed with the first, and we sat in silence on the bed. We endured plenty more silences over the next few weeks.

Aged 24, my biggest worry up till now had been getting the cash together to go travelling, but confirmation of her fertilised ovum burst through that worry like a pin into a balloon.

The front door banged open downstairs. My parents were home. We quickly made excuses and went to our favourite place for a talk: the pub. I ordered a pint and she a vodka. Just as the barmaid left, my girlfriend realised she couldn't drink anymore.

"How could we have been so stupid?" she asked.

Knowing was one thing, accepting another. I spent the next couple of weeks lying to friends, family and myself.

"What's wrong with you? You seem awfully quiet."

"Oh nothing, I'm just tired. Work is busy."

My girlfriend's family quickly spotted something was amiss. Normally full of conversation, she had practically stopped speaking to them.

One night after a wedding anniversary party for her

grandparents, my girlfriend's favourite aunt invited us back to the house for drinks.

Her husband poured a couple of large vodkas before leaving us alone with the aunt. She watched me gulp my drink nervously while my girlfriend barely sipped hers. Then she came out with it.

"Are you pregnant? Your Mam thinks you might be."

"I am, I' . . . "

The news seemed to gush right out of my girlfriend. My leg shook just listening to her.

"Relax honey," said her aunt. "It's OK."

A couple of days later I had to face up to her parents. Was her Mam going to ask me to leave the house? Would her father kick the shit out of me? I was summoned into the sitting room and asked to close the door. Her mother took a seat in the centre of the room while we sat on the couch, me pulling at the seams.

"This is not what I wanted for my daughter. It's not what I wanted for the two of you, but I would have been desperately, *desperately* disappointed if you hadn't told me sooner."

At the time, I would have been desperately relieved if we'd gone to England but like so many other things over the next few months, circumstances were manoeuvring beyond my control.

Her father's reaction was equally measured. He tapped me on the shoulder while I was eating dinner by myself at his house one evening.

"I just came over to say congratulations."

I didn't know it then, but that would be the last time I saw him alive.

My girlfriend was busy telling people, but I was still determined to reveal nothing. Saying she's pregnant solidified our situation; this baby was going to happen.

Mam had always warned me not to come back to this house "if you get someone pregnant or get an STD", while my father once explained to me why I should wait until I get married before having sex.

Time, nature and my girlfriend fought me, forced me to sit down on a sunny Sunday afternoon in April and wait for my parents to come home. I waited all afternoon and all evening. When I was about to go to bed, they returned.

"I've something to tell you," I said.

"We know, we know," said my Mam.

"She's preg-- what do you mean you know?"

My dad fell into a chair and scratched his grey hair while my mother circled the kitchen.

"I'm having a smoke, fuck it, I am having a smoke. Bryan, have one," said my Mam.

"I don't smoke, stop offering. Why are you reacting like that?"

"It's time for a family chat," she said. "We know because you're never here and when you are, you're in your room. But we love you, and we will support you."

"Dad?"

"I think what your mother said, but you shouldn't get married."

The conversation went on like that until I went to bed. It might have been unfair to confirm their fears while they were drunk (they told me so the next day). But this was about me getting the hardest bit over with.

At the time, my girlfriend and I worked in a service for people with intellectual disabilities, and one of the residents came down with chickenpox. Our manager called a meeting and detailed to the entire staff the complications it can cause in pregnant women.

"If any staff member is expecting a baby they need tell me."

"Sure who here is pregnant?" said a colleague.

"You never know!" said my boss.

Everyone laughed. I laughed the hardest.

The next day we revealed all to our manager, and a little later to everyone else. Then we left for a three-week holiday to South Africa where it wouldn't matter who knew I'd knocked up my girlfriend.

South Africa started badly. We had a big argument on the first night.

"I want you to take that test to find out if the baby has Down Syndrome."

"I'm not getting it and I wouldn't want to know if the baby had it. Why would you even ask?"

"We work in the area; you know how easily it can happen."

On the way back to the hotel she tried to put her arms around me, but I pulled away.

"Be like that."

She walked ahead of me and into the hotel.

I went to the bar and ordered two double vodkas and sat with an old drunk and guilt for company. I was asking because I didn't want any more surprises.

I wanted to get on with the rest of our twenties and go to Australia like everyone else. I finished the drinks, ordered another and went up to our room.

"I mentioned the test because I don't know how to handle this. It's not what I wanted or planned, and now all these people know. You don't seem to have any problems with it."

I explained until I cried. She told me it'd be OK. It would have to be.

We had plenty more arguments on that trip. Another finished with me running along a beach until there were sweat patches on my t-shirt. Near the water I prayed to God to help me make all of this all right.

I am not even that religious. I just liked the idea of having a dramatic moment – knee deep in the sea at the other end of the world – to replay like an old scene from *The Godfather*.

The day before we were due to fly home my girlfriend rang to see how her dad was doing. He'd been sick with cancer for months, but no one expected him to get worse.

"Dad is dying, we have to fly home tonight."

The next flight back to Dublin left from Johannesburg, and we flew up from Cape Town hoping to change our tickets.

J'Burg was a quicksand of panic. We ran from departures to arrivals, our luggage dragging behind like weights, fighting and failing to get out and home.

The airline staff delayed the plane and phoned the head office in Amsterdam, but they declared that we couldn't change our tickets for an earlier flight. The plane with its empty seats took off. So we checked into the Holiday Inn for the night.

My girlfriend rang her mother to explain. Her mother said to her there was no need to worry. Her father had already died. For her, this was the worst that could happen.

The next morning I walked in on her in the bathroom. The shower door was large and white, like a puppet screen, and the full black shadowy profile of her body revealed breasts that were filling and a normally flat belly swollen with a bump. I knew then we'd created a child.

My girlfriend went home and buried her dad. Afterwards, the pregnancy changed from something unplanned to a baby who "was meant to happen because it will bring some happiness back to my family."

This was grief and hope, and if there was nothing to be done about the former there was everything to arrange for the latter.

Hours before the doctor induced my girlfriend, we sat in the hospital waiting room. She flicked through a tattered copy of *Now* while I studied the waiting room.

An old man sat, perched on the edge of a chair, in the corner of the room.

A nurse approached.

"Are you Tracey's father?"

"I am," he said.

"Congratulations, she has just given birth to a baby girl."

The man stood and covered his mouth then sat down again before standing up and wiping his face with the back of his hand.

"Can I see her?"

The nurse smiled. I wanted to buy him a cigar.

"Why don't you sit down, and I'll tell her you're outside?"

An hour later, we were brought into the delivery ward and like a long car journey the day trundled on with the destination far from sight.

Every hour or so when the doctor came by, my girlfriend asked if she was 10 centimetres dilated yet – the point where the waiting stops, and the pushing starts – and he'd examine her before pronouncing, "a little longer."

The waiting was punctuated with walks up and down the corridor, as other expectant women shuffled past, holding their bellies, the steel hand rails or their anxious partners. My role was strictly supporting, and the entire day was a reminder that men should keep quiet in certain situations.

"Keep out of the way of the doctor but don't disappear altogether."

"No, you can't see if my waters are broken."

"Rub my back but stop fucking asking me if I'm all right."

Women can empathise about childbirth because they've biology on their side or have been through it themselves. The woman in the bed beside my girlfriend told her to be patient; she'd been here for two days. They both laughed.

For a man without medical training, it's an exercise in powerlessness. The only person interested in a father-to-be's opinions are the other expectant fathers, but they're too busy dealing with their expectant partners.

Delivering a baby forces a woman to shed all of her inhibitions and the father is expected to be there for it. The mother performs her most intimate acts under bright lights in front of her partner and a changing roster of nurses and doctors.

She's accosted with metallic instruments, tubes, gases and injections, told not to move and when to push. It's an unfathomably physical and emotional act that the producers of TV deliveries airbrush out when they have their glowing female leads squeeze out a sanitised baby in between commercial breaks.

My girlfriend pushed just three times to deliver Alex, but the entire labour took 14 hours. In the end, the baby slid right out. It seemed to me like a satisfying shit but what arrived was this quivering, purple and red angry mass. The nurse scooped the baby up and onto my girlfriend's chest.

"It's a boy."

Behold my most creative act.

Lots of men cry when their kids are born. It's an appropriate reaction, certainly more so than after a night out in Cape Town, but I couldn't. The last few months had left me numb – too many surprises, too many conversations and too many decisions.

"Would you like to cut the cord?"

I wielded the scissors – it was like cutting through old wet rope. The nurse cleaned the baby up before asking me to get him dressed (my clumsy fingers struggled for 15 minutes with the baby's bodysuit) and give him a bottle while she tended to my girlfriend. Afterwards, I phoned his grandparents and texted everyone else in my phone.

They were expecting news; I revealed it all over the phone, down the pub, in work and after football detailing the pushes, that he didn't even cry for the first hour and how his head had the human equivalent of new car smell depending on who was listening.

These were my first official fatherly acts, but it would be a while before I felt like a parent and the bond between us solidified. Some fathers might know straight away, but many don't and with good reason.

The mother physically bonds with her child for nine months. The mystified dad is handed a baby, offered congratulations and told it looks like him.

For weeks afterwards, I arrived home from a job I hated, saw the pram in the hall and wondered why we owned one. I worried about dying in a car accident or being electrocuted. I thought I was some kind of freak for being morbid when this should have been a happy time, but then a curious thing happened.

Over a few beers in a quiet pub one night, I explained to

a friend my problem. He was a few years older than me but had also just become a father for the first time.

"It gets you thinking about your own mortality," he said. "Babies make you realise how old you're getting, that you need to stop fooling around and provide for your family."

Creating a child laid bare my mortality. Death and birth are two sides of the same coin. By creating a child, I had flipped that coin. One part of my life had died, and another part was born.

In this new life, I had to do the work of providing and caring for my son. Back then, the work was feeding, winding and changing, and it pulled on me like a seamstress strengthening a double stitch until one day I was looking over a shitty nappy at someone I knew, and I couldn't tell what had come before.

My other job was to make sure whatever I did for the rest of my life counted, to do the work. The one thing I hadn't done up until that point was to write well, with passion and without holding back.

One night, when my girlfriend fell asleep, and after I'd fed the baby, I picked up the pen, and I looked at the blank page.

It was like gazing upon a lover for the first time.

We're Almost Out of Time

In the other chapters of this book, I shared practical tips for becoming more creative, but this chapter is different.

I shared my personal story because becoming a father is my most creative act, and my then girlfriend/now wife did the hard work.

I just had to learn to cut the cord from my old life and start a new one.

Years later, I still try to care, provide and set a good example for our son. I get it wrong all the time. I lose my temper; I set bad examples, and I say the wrong things, but that doesn't mean I can give up. You can't turn off being a parent.

Whether you are a parent or not, when you start your most important work an old part of your life will begin to die.

At first, this might frighten you, but that's OK. To create, you've got to let this old part of yourself go so a new part of your creative life can be born.

I don't know how many hours I have left and neither do you.

You and I could waste them by putting off our most important creative projects and by telling ourselves that we'll have time, tomorrow.

The painful reality is we might not, and if we keep putting things off, we will live a life of regret.

Don't get me wrong, I fall down, procrastinate and fail all the time, but I can see everyone's creative journey is different.

You already have everything you need inside you to become more creative. You just have to cut the cord on your past life and do your most important work.

We need your creative voice. Are you brave enough to speak?

Creative Takeaways

- Start today, because you're almost out of time.
- When you do, expect an old part of your life to fall away as a new part takes its place.

8

FALL FORWARDS

"If failure is not an option, then neither is success."
– Seth Godin

I've a confession to make.

I'm a failure. After I had turned 18, I spent four years training as a journalist in university. Upon graduating, I struggled to find meaningful work, and it took me a full year to find a low-paying job working as a reporter for a local newspaper in Dublin.

The news editor didn't like my stories, and she rewrote almost everything I sent her.

One dreary Wednesday evening, she pulled me aside and said, "I can't publish your main story this week Bryan; it wasn't good enough."

"What was wrong with it?" I asked.

"Your story was full of factual inaccuracies. If we'd published it, we could have been sued."

When she pointed out my mistakes, I conceded I'd failed

to research the news story properly.

As the weeks went on, I secretly resented her meddling with my stories, even though she was more experienced and talented than I was. I stuck it out for several months, but the low pay and my editor's way of working bothered me. So I handed in my notice.

I'd little tolerance for failure back then.

Next, I got a job working as a freelance sub-editor for *Sunday Tribune*. There, it was my job to write headlines and fix typos and grammar mistakes in the news and feature articles written by other journalists.

The chief sub-editor of *Sunday Tribune* took me aside one evening and pointed out the grammatical errors and typos I'd overlooked in a story that had almost gone to press.

"Bryan you need to be more careful. You're the last line of defence for these news stories," he said.

I vowed to try harder, to improve my skills and develop an eye for catching grammar mistakes, typos and factual errors. Over the course of several months, my skills improved, and I felt more confident about my craft.

One Sunday morning, I brewed a cup of coffee, opened the newspaper and began to read a supplement I'd sub-edited the day before.

Almost at once, I spotted it. There was a typo on a photo caption on the front page of the supplement. I punched the table, scrunched up the paper and threw my coffee down the sink.

Because I was a freelance sub-editor, the chief sub-editor didn't even have to let me go. Instead, he gave the work to someone more skilled. I would have done the same.

Afterwards, I had to pick myself up off the dirt and learn to move forwards.

I've failed, I've been rejected, and I've fallen down

repeatedly, but I've learnt that it pays to get up and move forwards. If you're determined to see your ideas through, you'll do the same.

When You Can't Reach the Top Shelf

You want to put your finished ideas on the top shelf for everyone to see, but when you reach up, your grasp doesn't extend far enough. To compound matters, the idea you're holding is chipped, and if you're honest, it's not good enough to sit on the top-shelf.

Perhaps you tried writing a story, but you can't bring it to a satisfying conclusion. Or maybe you started composing a musical masterpiece, but you don't know how to arrange the various pieces coherently. Or perhaps you set out to create the perfect clay pot only to have it to break apart in your hands.

Realising your reach exceeds your grasp and that you lack the skills to create an attractive idea is tough, but a ceramics teacher has an answer for you.

One day he was feeling experimental, so he divided his students into two groups. He asked the first group to create the perfect pot and graded them for the quality of their work. Then, the teacher asked the second group to create as many pots as possible and graded for the quantity of the output.

The ceramics teacher discovered the second group had more to show for their efforts *and* their pots were of a higher quality than the group who spent all their creative energy perfecting a single pot.

The group that laboured over creating the perfect pot

didn't improve their skills as quickly as the group that focused on producing pot after pot and learning from their chipped and ugly mistakes.

Photographer and author David Bayles and teacher and writer Ted Orland recount this story in their book *Art and Fear*,

 Art is human; error is human; ergo, art is error. Inevitably, your work . . . will be flawed. Why? Because you're a human being, and only human beings, warts and all, make art."

You can overcome your lack of skill if you're prepared to create a few ugly pots along the way.

If your first album flopped, record a second and a third. If your first book wasn't good enough, write a better one. If they said your film was boring, make a more exciting one.

Whatever you do, don't spend all your time perfecting a single idea, because if this pot cracks and shatters, you'll have nothing to show for your hard work.

I've written dozens of unpublished and rejected short stories and articles. Time and again, I've tried to write something worthwhile and found myself lacking.

Several years ago, I pushed my writing in a different direction. Instead, of working solely on short stories and journalism news articles, I set up a blog and wrote my first post.

I've always considered myself techy (My friends say nerdy!), but blogging was a new medium, and I quickly found my reach exceeded my grasp. Almost nobody read my early blog posts, and the few readers I found didn't stay long on my website.

Watching my pots smash on the ground was tough, and I thought of giving up writing online, deleting my blog and going back to fiction.

I couldn't do it.

There was something about being able to press "Publish" and seeing my words appear online that got me high because up until this point I had to wait for an editor or another gatekeeper to say my writing was good enough.

I don't know about you, but I hate asking for permission.

I consumed the works of other online writers and bloggers, and I discovered online readers consume information differently from readers of books.

The former has little time or patience; they scan articles and prefer if they're broken up with sub-headings, bullet points and images. The latter prefers more meaty and substantial pieces and has more patience for longer paragraphs.

After this lesson, I was able to create better-looking pots and put them on shelves higher up.

I found out how to source and create images for my posts so they were more pleasing for people to read, and I learnt how to promote posts online so that people could find them. I also taught myself basics of HTML and CSS, so I could customise the look and feel of my blog without spending money hiring a developer.

I used each lesson to improve my pots and to put them higher and higher. I'm not able to reach the top shelf yet, but my reach extends further than several years ago, and I feel better about my chipped pots because each one contains a chance to improve.

When You Create It (and They Don't Come)

A friend and I were sitting in a bar the other day, and over beer, potato wedges and mayonnaise, she was telling me about when she learnt to surf in San Francisco Bay.

Being particularly uncoordinated, I don't surf, but I've always loved the water. It was a wet and miserable Thursday evening in Dublin, and I was happy to listen to her stories from a (slightly) warmer place.

She told me about her unhappy friend from San Francisco.

Surfer guy had quit his boring job in a grey office to sell surfboards. He was supposed to be living his dream, but things weren't working out for him.

"My friend spends his days carving and tailoring grain surfboards for his customers," she said. "He spends hours varnishing the boards and painting these intricate and personal designs. People love them!"

She showed me a picture of a slender, polished surfboard.

"If I could surf, that's the board I'd buy," I said.

"You've never used a surfboard this good," said my friend, unaware that I'd never used a surfboard at all. "He puts so much passion and care into his designs that they remind me of art. They're more expensive than normal surfboards but his customers don't care."

"Why isn't your friend happy?" I asked. "Does he miss the 9-to-5 grind?"

"He can't make a living off his surfboards," she said. "Nobody is buying them. His shop is empty."

"I thought you said they are like art and that they cost more than regular surfboards?"

"They are, they do, but he doesn't like going out and marketing his boards," she said. "He believes they're good enough to sell by themselves and the idea of marketing his art makes him feel icky."

I sipped my beer and wondered what writer and marketer Seth Godin (b. 1960) would think of surfer guy and his reluctance to market his fantastic product. Godin once wrote,

> If you don't get noticed, you're invisible. You can't tell a story and your marketing ends there and then. The story you'll need to tell in order to get noticed must match the worldview of the people you're telling it to, and it has to be clear and obvious."

Surfer guy has a great product, and he believes his boards should succeed because he's worked hard at creating something great.

Unfortunately, he's mistaken.

Surfer-guy needs to go out into the world, find his would-be customers and tell them a story about his hand-crafted boards, how they will help them become a different sort of surfer in a way that just isn't possible with any old mass-produced board.

He needs to tell his would-be customers that, like them, he lives and breathes the open water, and he puts love and effort into creating a personal, unique surfboard that they'll treasure.

Many artists say they find marketing their work sleazy. They mistakenly believe marketing isn't something they should engage in because their work should speak for itself.

Remember that successful authors go on book tours, filmmakers arrange press screenings and musicians send copies of their work to music journalists and writers.

In an ideal world, artists wouldn't have to market their work, but you're competing for attention alongside Netflix, Xbox, Playstation, Spotify, the cinema, television, YouTube, among others.

The internet is a great leveller, and the millions of artists and creators around the world have access to mostly the same resources as you.

It's great that everybody can get into the party, but because we're all in the same room, it's up to you to mingle and win people's attention.

Nobody is going to do it for you unless you can afford to hire someone to market your work or you have a traditional deal with an editor, record company or film studio.

Does marketing your ideas make you feel icky? When was the last time you told somebody about your creative work?

If you believe your work is good enough, and your audience should notice your ideas, you'll find it almost impossible to attract an audience.

You must go out and tell stories about your creative work. Don't be shy or embarrassed about this. If you're proud of what you've created and you know it's good, it's your duty to tell people about it.

Consider the message of your creative project. Are you using language, materials and a medium that your target audience is familiar with?

If you don't get comfortable telling stories about your surfboards, music, writing or your most important creative work, you'll struggle to find an audience for your work.

When You Lack Courage

It's a warm afternoon in July, and you're sitting in a walled-garden in a comfortable foldout chair with a cool drink. The garden is in full bloom, and it's protected by a stone wall so tall that you can't see over it.

You can hear the faint sound of someone calling to you from beyond the wall, but they're too far away to make out. There's a rickety wooden ladder against the wall, and you debate about climbing to see who is on the other side and find out what they want.

But it'd be so much easier to stay in the garden, sip your drink, enjoy the sunshine and forget about the voice calling to you.

Most people stay in the garden because it's the sensible thing to do, but your idea is out there, calling to you.

Do you have the courage to seek it out?

Perhaps you've become so attached to a way of doing things, to sitting in your comfortable chair, that you fail to move on long after the sun has set.

Maybe you recognise the voice calling to you as bold and inspired, but you're afraid of what you'll find if you go all the way over, so you stay where you are.

Perhaps you have the talents and abilities to scale the peak of any creative project, but instead of working up a sweat, you squander your gifts for a comfortable life.

Worst of all, instead of taking a break from your book, painting or album to sit for a while, you quit your craft, vowing never to climb that wall again.

Henry Ford (1863-1947) wasn't content to sit in the garden.

The voice calling to him was an idea for an inexpensive, prototype car that he could sell to consumers. In 1899, he formed the Detroit Automobile Company with financial backing from a Detroit businessman named William H. Murphy.

Ford's early versions of the car were too heavy and expensive, so his backers dissolved the company, taking away Ford's ladder.

Ford tried again and formed the Henry Ford Company. Developing a prototype car was an expensive affair, and again his backers lost patience with the mounting costs and delays and took away Ford's ladder.

Instead of quitting, Ford considered the wall he was laying his ladder against. He realised he was working with financial backers who were too hands-on.

He also believed he'd made enough mistakes with his earlier prototypes to see his idea through and create a model he could sell. All he needed was the financial support from the right investor.

Instead of quitting, Ford approached Alexander Malcomson, a coal dealer from Detroit and asked him for financial backing to finish his prototype car.

Malcomson agreed.

Now working under a more independent business model, Ford built an assembly plant for his car and oversaw every aspect of it.

Finally, he created, built and shipped the lightest car of its time, the Model A. The Ford Motor Company began manufacturing 15 of these popular cars a day, and in 1904 it expanded operations to cater to a demanding public.

Although Malcomson and Ford later fell out, Ford is regarded as one of history's most creative industrialists.

It would have been easier for Ford to quit, but he had the courage to see his idea through.

He said about failure:

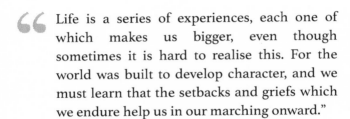

> Life is a series of experiences, each one of which makes us bigger, even though sometimes it is hard to realise this. For the world was built to develop character, and we must learn that the setbacks and griefs which we endure help us in our marching onward."

Remember, when you encounter an obstacle, it's there to challenge you and stretch your abilities because if it were easy, it wouldn't be worth doing. Now onwards!

Learning from Failure

A failed creative project is tough to swallow, but it provides you with a great chance to learn more about yourself and your craft.

All you have to do is ask the right questions about what you gained and lost and then capture and apply these lessons before you begin your next work. The following series of questions explain how to do just that, and you should ask them at the end of a big creative project.

Assessing Your Creative Gains

- What have I learnt about my needs and preferences/my audience's needs and preferences?
- Should I change any of my assumptions or ideas? Did this project reveal the spark of an idea for some future work?
- What insight did I gain into my chosen subject and how should I adjust my approach to it?

- What have I discovered about the way that I work and about myself? How effective is my current creative process?
- How did I grow my artistic skills? Did this creative project increase my abilities in some way, or did it expose a weakness in my skillset I must address?

Calculating Your Creative Losses

- What was the direct cost of my work or idea in terms of time, financial resources and missed opportunities?
- Did I hurt my reputation in some way with my audience?
- Did this project consume too much of my attention? Did it reduce my confidence?

Summary

- What are the key insights and takeaways from my creative project?

Failure: Your Key to Creative Mastery

I spent most of my twenties working as a freelance journalist for newspapers, magazines and even a national radio station.

I slowly learnt how to avoid my mistakes, but I still struggled to earn a living out of this strange profession.

So one day, I applied for a job as a care worker. Then I

gathered my portfolio of press clippings, drove to the nearest dump and threw them into the skip.

After failing as a journalist, I worked in healthcare as a care-worker and then later in the technology industry as a copywriter and marketer.

The healthcare profession has little tolerance for failure because if you fail somebody gets sick or gets hurt. (Thankfully I wasn't involved in any failures like these!)

The technology industry has a greater tolerance for failure, as you can release a software patch that fixes the bugs in your product or even change the direction of the product or service altogether.

Although I couldn't see it then, failing as a journalist opened up the door to succeeding at other kinds of writing.

Whatever industry you work in, learning from failure takes guts, and if you're walking the creative path, your courage will be tested many times.

You must move forward, though. If you find this a struggle, take heart. American writer Truman Capote said, "Failure is the condiment that gives success its flavour."

Instead of ruminating about cracked pots, the critics and your talents (or lack thereof), use your low points as learning experiences.

Each time you stumble, consider what you can take from the experience. Consider how you can fall forwards and create something new, something better.

Creative Takeaways

- The next time you fail, extract painful lessons from the project and apply what you can.

- Haven't failed recently? Beware! You're becoming complacent. It's time to learn a creative skill and put it to use.

9

SHIPPING YOUR MOST IMPORTANT WORK

"That mid-way haven is called 1,000 True Fans. It is an alternate destination for an artist to aim for."
– Kevin Kelly

Is it scribbled on an old yellow notebook? Did you bury it in the bottom drawer beneath a stack of papers in your study? Or do you tell people about it only over a cold beer on a hot, late summer's evening?

If you're not finishing little ideas every day, you're doing your work (and your audience) a disservice.

You must accumulate hundreds and thousands of finished little ideas until they bond together and possess a life of their own.

It sounds exhausting.

I know you don't have enough time. Or money. Or energy.

But that's OK because creativity thrives when you impose limits on your ideas (see Book 2).

Figuring out how to publish a book, record an album or put together a collection when you're coming up short will help you focus on what matters. It'll help you overcome the nasty vice of perfectionism and get more of your work out into the world.

A deadline might loom like a guillotine, but you can harness this stress to take action and ship your work before the blade drops.

But what if you fail?

What if people reject your ideas, or you look at your finished work and know deep down it's a shadow of what you imagined?

Creative masters face these problems too.

Instead of putting away their pen, brush, camera or guitar, they seek out new and better ways to fail faster. They learn from their mistakes. They learn from their craft. And they learn from their audience.

They plunge the hot steel of their ideas into a cold bucket of water where it either solidifies into something lasting or it cracks and falls apart.

Creative masters test their ideas in the real world, act on critical feedback and use what they've learnt to ship something new, something better.

The good news is you don't need to be a genius like Mozart or have the resources of Tharp to learn from your audience.

Blog, use social media, reach out to artists you admire, share pictures of your work on Instagram, upload clips to YouTube, and gauge how people react.

Show drafts of your book, album or art to an inner circle and get constructive critical feedback.

The free tools and resources at your disposal are more powerful and far-reaching than anything past creative masters dreamt of. You don't even need to reach that many people.

Writer and author Kevin Kelly (b. 1952) popularised a maxim that an artist today needs only 1,000 true fans to earn a living.

 "A true fan is defined as 'a fan who will buy anything you produce.' These diehard fans will drive 200 miles to see you sing; they will buy the hardback and paperback and audio versions of your book; they will purchase your next figurine, sight unseen...

If you have roughly 1,000 fans like this (also known as superfans), you can make a living— if you are content to make a living, but not a fortune."

So forget about the blockbuster hit or selling out a football stadium. Leave that for the reality TV stars, for those with million dollar contracts, for those who were picked.

Going deep into your work isn't about being picked; it's about finishing an idea because you believe in it.

So, build relationships with just 1,000 people who will drive to your exhibitions, attend your openings, look for signed copies of your work and buy anything you create.

You'll reach your 1,000 true fans faster if you learn just a little about marketing your art. If the idea of "marketing" feels like you're wearing a pair of itchy underpants, ask yourself: Do I believe in my big idea?

I want you to believe.

I want you to reframe what you're about to do next – you know, marketing – as storytelling. Go out into the wider world and tell people stories about what you've done and how your ideas will add value to their lives in some small way.

I want you to know this is your responsibility.

Don't buy into to the cliché of the lone starving artist who violates his or her pipeline to God (or the creative muse) by accepting a paycheque.

Doctors, architects and engineers are highly paid for their hard work and years of training and experience; nobody expects them to work for free.

If you ship, if you add value to people's lives, you deserve to be paid what you're worth.

Once you start earning money from your work, use it to serve your new audience, to acquire the resources you need or even to work on your passion project.

What you ship today should inspire what you create tomorrow. It should give you the freedom and confidence to create something new, something grander or even something more intimate.

In the end, when your little ideas bond into a big idea and take on a life of their own and you know you held nothing back, you'll feel a sense of accomplishment that outlasts any material reward.

You'll understand what it is to create.

AFTERWORD

If you enjoyed this series, rate this book and leave a short review. Reviews like yours help me write more books like this one.

Finally, if you have feedback about this book you can always email bryan@becomeawritertoday.com. I'd love to hear from you.

WAIT!

DID YOU CLAIM YOUR FREE BONUS?

VISIT
becomeawritertoday.com/pocbonus

ACKNOWLEDGMENTS

Thanks to Command+Z Content and Beth Crosby for their great editing and Martine Ellis for proof-reading. Thanks to Terri Black for the book cover design. And finally, thank you for reading.

ABOUT THE AUTHOR

In this life, Bryan Collins is an author.

In another life, he worked as a journalist and a radio producer. Before that, he plucked chickens. He is passionate about helping people accomplish more with their writing projects, and when he's not writing, he's running.

At becomeawritertoday.com, Bryan offers new writers practical advice about writing, creativity, productivity and more. His work has appeared on *Fast Company*, *Lifehacker* and *Copyblogger*.

Bryan holds a degree in communications and journalism, a diploma in social care, a master's degree in disability studies and a diploma in digital media.

You can reach him on Twitter @BryanJCollins, via email at bryan@becomeawritertoday.com or join his Become a Writer Today Facebook page.

Bryan is also the author of the novella *Poor Brother, Rich Brother* and a three-part series: *Become a Writer Today*.

He lives an hour outside of Dublin.

becomeawritertoday.com
bryan@becomeawritertoday.com

TOOLS FOR BECOMING MORE CREATIVE

Below is a list of tools I use and rely on as a writer and blogger.

I've also included some other recommended resources that will help you with your creative work.

The list is relatively long and (depending on the nature of your creative work) you won't need to use all of these tools.

Remember, the creative process and your ideas are more important than any tool.

99designs

In the past, I've used 99designs to find a designer to create a book cover for one of my books. If you want a professional design (like a logo, t-shirt, business card or packaging) for your online business, 99designs is a good place to start.

A smartphone

The best camera is the one you have with you at the time, and if you need to take a picture or just capture an idea, your smartphone is almost always the best choice. I use an iPhone.

A whiteboard

I keep a large whiteboard next to where I write. It's a great way of capturing and organising ideas. I also use it for mind maps and for creating outlines for articles, chapters and even books. I find a whiteboard less confining that traditional digital tools.

Audible

As a creative person, your inputs (what you read, listen to and watch) are just as important as your outputs (what you write, paint or draw). I spend at least an hour a day listening to audiobooks that I purchased from <u>Audible</u> on my smartphone. If you sign up, they'll give you your first audiobook for free.

Behance

A showcase site for design and other creative work. Behance is great for inspiration and also for finding designers to work with. Also, see Dribble.

Brain.FM

<u>Brain.FM</u> provides AI-generated music for focus, relaxation and deep work. When I use this, I find I can enter a state of creative flow faster. Plug in a pair of headphones and you're good to go.

Buffer

I use <u>Buffer</u> to share articles, photos and social media updates by myself and others on Instagram, Facebook, LinkedIn, Twitter and Pinterest. Buffer simplifies sharing social media updates across multiple networks and enables you to schedule your updates in advance.

You can also collaborate with others and enable them to manage your social media profiles... leaving you more time to work on your creative projects. More advanced social media users should consider Meet Edgar.

Canva

For years, I used Photoshop and the rest of the Adobe Suite to create images. Today, I rely on Canva because it simplifies creating images using a drag-and-drop editor.

Creative Commons

This site will help you legally share your work online and find a license or copyright that suits your business model, website or project.

The site's search tool will also help you find images, music and other media that you can use in your creative projects, commercial or otherwise.

Dragon Dictate

I use Dragon software to dictate early drafts of blog posts, book chapters and articles. This piece of software enables me to write faster, and it also reduces the amount of time I spend struggling with repetitive strain injury (RSI). In this article, I explain how to get started with dictation.

Evernote

If I have an idea that I don't want to forget, I keep it in here. I also save articles I like into Evernote as part of my personal swipe file. Sometimes, I take photos of mind maps on my whiteboard with my phone and put them in Evernote too. It's my digital brain.

Image sites

Gratisography contains awesome and free high-resolution photos you can use for your creative projects, as does All The Free Stock and Death to the Stock.

I recommend Depositphotos for premium stock images. You could also take the images yourself and apply an Instagram filter. Designers can get icons on The Noun Project.

Freedom

If you keep getting distracted while writing, use the app Freedom. It will disable your internet access for a pre-determined period, allowing you to focus on writing and not on cat videos!

Grammarly

If you need help proofing your work, I always recommend you hire a proofreader. However, I also recommend Grammarly as another line of defence and for checking your writing as you go.

Google Docs

I use Google Docs to write on the go and to track my progress in spreadsheets. I also collaborate with other writers and creative professionals, and *it's free*.

G Suite (formerly Google Apps for Work)

It's time to put the hard-drives and USB keys away. Essentially, G Suite enables me to send and receive emails from the BecomeAWriterToday.com domain (bryan[at]BecomeAWriterToday.com) using the Gmail interface.

I also get lots of additional cloud storage and can easily

collaborate with other writers, editors and designers. This isn't free, but it's affordable.

Headline Analyzer

This free online tool will check your headlines and give you practical tips for improving them so they are more emotional and captivating. Alternatively, consider CoSchedule Headline Analyzer.

Headspace

This is my meditation app of choice. If you've never meditated before, Andy Puddicombe will teach you the basics through guided lessons. I also suggest searching for Tara Brach's free guided meditations online.

Hemingway App

If you're not a confident writer, don't worry. This app will review your text and, in the spirit of Ernest Hemingway, it will tell you what to remove or edit so your writing is bold and clear.

Kindle Spy

KindleSpy is a great tool that will help you see which books are selling on Amazon and how much they earn. Then you can use this information to increase sales of your book.

LeadPages

I use LeadPages to create landing and squeeze pages for my books. I also use it to create sign-up forms for my mailing list.

Your bed or chair of choice

Fact: Napping is conducive to creativity. Just ask Salvador Dali. The trick is to wake yourself up after 20 minutes so you avoid going into a deep sleep. Then when you wake, get straight to work.

Noise cancelling headphones and an album of instrumental music

A good set of noise cancelling headphones will help you concentrate on your work no matter where you are. Each morning, I don my pair and listen to albums like "Rain for Sleeping and Relaxation" on repeat while I write.

(Yes, that album is exactly like the name sounds.)

iMindMap/MindNode/MindMeister

I've used these affordable tools to create mind maps in the past. They're easy to learn too. Alternatively, you can create a mind map using pen and paper.

Medium

Do you just want to write and share your ideas online, but you're not interested in running a blog? Medium removes all of the technical challenges of blogging and helps you connect with readers.

Oblique Strategies

In 1975, the producer and musician Brian Eno and the artist and painter Peter Schmidt created a deck of cards that give musicians and artists constraints within which to work.

These constraints foster the kind of lateral thinking creativity demands. Essentially, you draw a card at random from the deck and are presented with a prompt like: 'Do the words need changing?'

You can buy the deck or use a free, web-version.

Pilot G4 Pen and a Moleskine notebook

No, there's no need to use a Moleskine notebook for writing or capturing ideas, but I'm drawn to the build quality of these notebooks and the feel of the paper. I've a box full of these near where I write.

Even if you're not drawn to these admittedly expensive notebooks, working on your ideas with a pen (you can't go wrong with the Pilot G4) and paper will liberate fresh thinking.

Screenflow for Mac

This is a great tool for recording video and screencasts. It's also relatively simple to edit your recordings and export them to a format suitable for Facebook, YouTube or your website. Also consider Camtasia.

Scrivener

I can't recommend Scrivener enough. I use it to write blog posts and books. I've used Scrivener to write feature articles for newspapers, reports, ebooks, a thesis and even a novel.

>> Get my free blogging template.

Other useful writing apps include Ulysses, Pages and IA Writer.

Sumo

Sumo is an all-in-one tool that enables you to gather email addresses, set up a share bar on the side of blog posts and also track how people interact with your work online. If you're sharing your work online, I highly recommended it.

Upwork

No matter how talented or hard-working you are, it's impossible to do everything alone. UpWork is a great service for finding designers, editors and more who can help you with time-consuming tasks so you can spend more time on your book, art or music.

I've used Upwork to hire video-editors and developers who fixed problems on my website.

Web-hosting

For your author website or blog, I suggest hosting with Siteground. If you need help, check out my detailed guide on how to start a blog: https://becomeawritertoday.com/start-a-blog/

GET THE BECOME A WRITER TODAY SERIES

Yes, You Can Write!
101 Proven Writing Prompts that Will Help You Find Creative Ideas Faster for Your Journal, Blogging, Writing Your Book and More
(Book 1)

The Savvy Writer's Guide to Productivity
How to Work Less, Finish Writing Your Story or Book, and Find the Success You Deserve
(Book 2)

The Art of Writing a Non-Fiction Book
An Easy Guide to Researching, Creating, Editing, and Self-Publishing Your First Book
(Book 3)

http://becomeawritertodaybook.com

REFERENCES

Books

Altucher, James. *Choose Yourself,* James Altucher, 2013.

Bales, David and Orland, Ted. *Art and Fear.* Image Continuum Press. 2001.

Campbell Joseph and Moyers, Bill. *The Power of Myth,* Anchor Books. 1998.

Catmull, Ed. *Creativity Inc.: Overcoming The Unforeseen Forces That Stand in the Way of True Inspiration.* Random House. 2014.

Csikzentmihalyi, Mihaly. *Flow: The Psychology of Happiness.* Ebury Publishing, 2002.

Covey, Stephen R. *The 7 Habits of Highly Effective People.* Free Press. 1989.

Dali, Salvador. *50 Secrets of Magic Craftsmanship.* Dover Publications. 1992.

De Bono, Edward. *How to Have a Beautiful Mind.* Ebury Press. 2008.

Duhigg, Charles. *The Power of Habit: Why We Do What We Do In Life and Business.* Random House. 2012.

Ferriss, Timothy. *Tools of Titans: The Tactics, Routines, and Habits of Billionaires, Icons, and World-Class Performers*. Ebury Publishing. Kindle Edition. 2016.

Gelb, Michael. *How To Think Like Leonardo da Vinci: Seven Steps to Boosting Your Everyday Genius*. Harper Collins. 2009.

Gladwell, Malcolm. *Outliers: The Story of Success*. Back Bay Books. 2011.

Godin, Seth. *Tribes*. Hachette Digital. 2008.

Godin, Seth. *All Marketers Are Liars*. Portfolio. 2012.

Green, Robert. *Mastery*. Viking. 2012.

Gregoire, Carolyn and Kaufmann, Scott Barry. *Wired to Create: Unraveling the Mysteries of the Creative Mind*. Tarcher-Perigee. 2015.

Harris, Sam. *Waking Up: A Guide to Spirituality Without Religion*. Simon & Schuster. 2014.

Isaacson, Walter. *Einstein: His Life and Universe*. Simon & Schuster. 2008.

Isaacson, Walter. *Steve Jobs: The Exclusive Biography*. Machete Digital. 2011.

Kahneman, Daniel. *Thinking, Fast and Slow*. Farrer, Straus and Giroux. 2011.

King, Stephen. *On Writing Well: A Memoir of the Craft*. Hodder and Stoughton. 2010.

Kleon, Austin. *Show Your Work*. Workman Publishing Company. 2014.

Kleon, Austin. *Steal Like an Artist*. Workman Publishing Company. 2012.

Levy, Mark. *Accidental Genius: Using Writing to Generate Your Best Ideas, Insight and Content* (Second Edition). Berrett-Koehler Publishers. 2009.

Newport, Cal. *Deep Work: Rules for Focus in a Distracted World*. Piatkus. 2016.

Rodriguez, Robert. *Rebel Without a Crew.* Plume. 1995.

Reis, Eric. *The Lean Startup: How Today's Entrepreneurs Use Continuous Innovation to Create Radically Successful Businesses.* Crown Business. 2011.

Segal, Zoe Gillian. *Getting There.* Harry N. Abrams. 2015.

Tharp, Twyla. *The Creative Habit: Learn It and Use It For Life.* Simon & Schuster. 2014.

T.S. Eliot. *The Sacred Wood: Essays on Poetry and Criticism.* Bartleby.com. 2009.

Waitzkin, Josh. *The Art of Learning: An Inner Journey to Optimal Performance.* Free Press. 2007.

Wilboue, Edwin Charles. *Victor Hugo By A Witness Of His Life.* 2007. Accessed at https://archive.org/stream/victorhugobyawit003274mbp/victorhugobyawit003274mbp_djvu.txt on March 15, 2016

Audio, Videos and Films

The American Reader. *This Day In Lettres: 3 April (1855): Charles Dickens to Maria Winter.* Accessed at http://theamericanreader.com/3-april-1855-charles-dickens-to-maria-winter/ on May 22, 2016.

Cleese, John. *Lecture On Creativity for Video Arts.* 1991. Accessed at https://www.youtube.com/watch?v=Qbyoed4aVpo on November 22, 2015.

Ferris, Tim. *The "Wizard" of Hollywood, Robert Rodriguez.* Four Hour Work Week. 2015. Accessed at The Tim Ferris Experiment http://fourhourworkweek.com/2015/08/23/the-wizard-of-hollywood-robert-rodriguez/ on November 22, 2015.

Greenberg, Robert. *Great Masters: Mozart-His Life and Music.* The Great Courses. 2013.

Pink, Daniel. *The Puzzle of Motivation.* 2009. Accessed at

TED http://www.ted.com/talks/dan_pink_on_motiva-tion/transcript?language=en on November 22, 2015.

Lasseter, John et al. *Toy Story*. Pixar Studios. 1995.

Lasseter, John et. al. *Toy Story 2*. Pixar Studios. 2000.

Lucas, George et al. *Star Wars: A New Hope*. Lucasfilm. 1977.

Kershner, Irvin et al. *Star Wars: The Empire Strikes Back*. Lucasfilm. 1980.

Jobs, Steve. *iPhone 2007 Presentation (Full HD)*. Accessed at https://www.youtube.com/watch?v=vN4U5FqrOdQ on December 4. 2015.

Articles, Research Papers and Essays

Altmann, E. M. & Trafton, J.G. *Task interruption: Resumption lag and the role of cues.* Department of Psychology. Michigan State University. 2004.

Asimov, Isaac. *How Do People Get New Ideas? MIT Technology review.* 2014. Accessed at https://www.technologyreview.com/s/531911/isaac-asimov-asks-how-do-people-get-new-ideas/ on April 17, 2016.

Baird, Benjamin et. al. *Inspired by Distraction: Mind Wandering Facilitates Creative Incubation.* Psychological Science. 2011. Accessed at http://pss.sagepub.com/content/early/2012/08/31/0956797612446024.abstract on May 9, 2016.

Brogan, Jan. *When being distracted is a good thing.* The Boston Globe. 2012. Accessed at https://www.bostonglobe.com/lifestyle/health-wellness/2012/02/27/when-being-distracted-good-thing/1AYWPlDplqluMEPrWHe5sL/story.html on May 22, 2016.

Clear, James. T*he Akrasia Effect: Why We Don't Follow Through on What We Set Out to Do (And What to Do About It).*

2016. Accessed at http://jamesclear.com/akrasia on March 15, 2016.

Coyle, Danie. *A Gauge for Measuring Effective Practice*. The Talent Code. Daniel, Coyle. 2009. Accessed at http://thetalentcode.com/2011/05/31/a-gauge-for-measuring-effective-practice/ on May 9, 2016.

Dumas D, Dunbar KN. *The Creative Stereotype Effect*. PLOS. 2016. Accessed at http://journals.plos.org/plosone/article?id=10.1371/journal.pone.0142567 on May 22, 2016.

Ericsson, Anders K. et al. *The Role of Deliberate Practice in Acquisition of Expert Performance*. American Psychology Association. 1993.

Howie, Hugh. *My advice to aspiring authors*. The Way Finder. 2013. Accessed at http://www.hughhowey.com/my-advice-to-aspiring-authors/ on June 24, 2016.

Kageyama, Noa. *The Most Valuable Lesson I Learned from Playing the Violin*. The Creativity Post. 2012. Accessed at http://www.creativitypost.com/arts/the_most_valuable_-lesson_i_learned_from_playing_the_violin on May 22, 2016.

Kelly, Kevin. *1,000 True Fans*. The Technium. 2008. Accessed at http://kk.org/thetechnium/1000-true-fans/ on June 24, 2016.

Herbert, Wray. *Ink on Paper: Some Notes on Note Taking*. Association for Psychological Science. 2014. Accessed at http://www.psychologicalscience.org/index.php/news/were-only-human/ink-on-paper-some-notes-on-note-taking.html on May 22, 2016.

Mac Kinnon, Donald. *The Identification of Creativity*. Applied Psychology. 1963.

Mueller, Pam and Oppenheimer, Daniel. *The Pen Is Mightier Than the Keyboard: Advantages of Longhand Over Laptop Note Taking*. 2014. Accessed at https://sites.udel.edu/victorp/files/2010/11/Psychological-Science-2014-Mueller-

0956797614524581-1u0hoyu.pdf on May 22, 2016. Association for Psychological Science.

Oakley, Keith and Djikic, Maja. *How Reading Transforms Us*. New York Times. 2014. Accessed at *http://www.nytimes.com/2014/12/21/opinion/sunday/how-writing-transforms-us.html?_r=0* on September 15, 2015.

Reader's Digest. *The Charles Goodyear Story*. Good Year. 1957. Accessed at *Good Year Corporate*. Accessed at *https://corporate.goodyear.com/en-US/about/history/charles-goodyear-story.html* on November 22, 2015.

Reis, Eric. *How DropBox Started As A Minimal Viable Product*. 2011. Accessed at http://techcrunch.com/2011/10/19/dropbox-minimal-viable-product/ on April 17, 2016.

Schwartz and Porath. *Why You Hate Work*. The New York Times. 2014. Accessed at http://www.nytimes.com/2014/06/01/opinion/sunday/why-you-hate-work.html on February 22, 2016.

Sternberg, Jacques. *In Act 2, the TV Hit Man Becomes a Pitch Man*. The New York Times. 2007. Accessed at http://www.nytimes.com/2007/07/18/arts/television/18madm.html?_r=0 on May 22, 2016.

Walker, Tim. *The Telegraph. Ernest Hemingway never wrote drunk, says granddaughter Mariel Hemingway*. The Telegraph. 2013. Accessed at http://www.telegraph.co.uk/culture/books/booknews/10236200/Ernest-Hemingway-never-wrote-drunk-says-granddaughter-Mariel-Hemingway.html on September 15, 2015.

Wilson, Timothy D et al. *Just think: The challenges of the disengaged mind*. Science Mag. 2014.

Vaynerchuk, Gary. *3 Ways You Need To Be Marketing Your Book in 2015*. Gary Vaynerchuk. 2016. Accessed at https://www.garyvaynerchuk.com/3-ways-you-need-to-be-marketing-your-book-in-2015/ on June 24, 2016.

Ying, Jon. *Meet the Team! (Part 1)*. Dropbox, 2009. Accessed at https://blogs.dropbox.com/dropbox/2009/02/meet-the-team-part-1/ on June 24, 2016.